The Kids' Book of GREAT CITIES

CHARLES CONWAY

SQUARE and CIRCUS

KU-276-923

The Kids' Book of GREAT CITIES

First published in the UK
in 2014 by

SQUARE AND CIRCUS
3 Sterne Close
Cambridge
CB1 3RA
UK

All rights reserved. No part of this publication
may be reproduced, stored in or introduced into a
retrieval system, or transmitted in any form or by
any means (electronic, mechanical, photocopying,
recording or otherwise) without the prior written
permission of both the copyright owner and the
publisher of this book.

Text © CHARLES CONWAY
Illustrations © SUPRIYA SAHAI

Printed in Italy by L.E.G.O. SPA

ISBN 9780957533738

www.squareandcircus.co.uk

Images:
SHUTTERSTOCK and
Anky / Anton Oparin / Antony McAulay / Catwalker / Chungking / Dominik
Michalek / Haider Y Abdulla / Haris Vythoulkas / Holbox / Jess Yu / Jose
Ignacio Soto / Kris Yeager / LIUSHENGFILM / Marco Rubino / Matej Kastelic /
Melodia plus photos / Migel / Milosk50 / Neale Cousland / Neftali / Nimon
/ Oleksiy Mark / Philip Bird LRPS CPAGB / Pius Lee / Polina Shestakova /
Semmick Photo / Tooykrub / Visun Khankasem / Welcomia / Yabu

The Kids' Book of

GREAT CITIES

Times Square in New York City is called the Crossroads of the World!

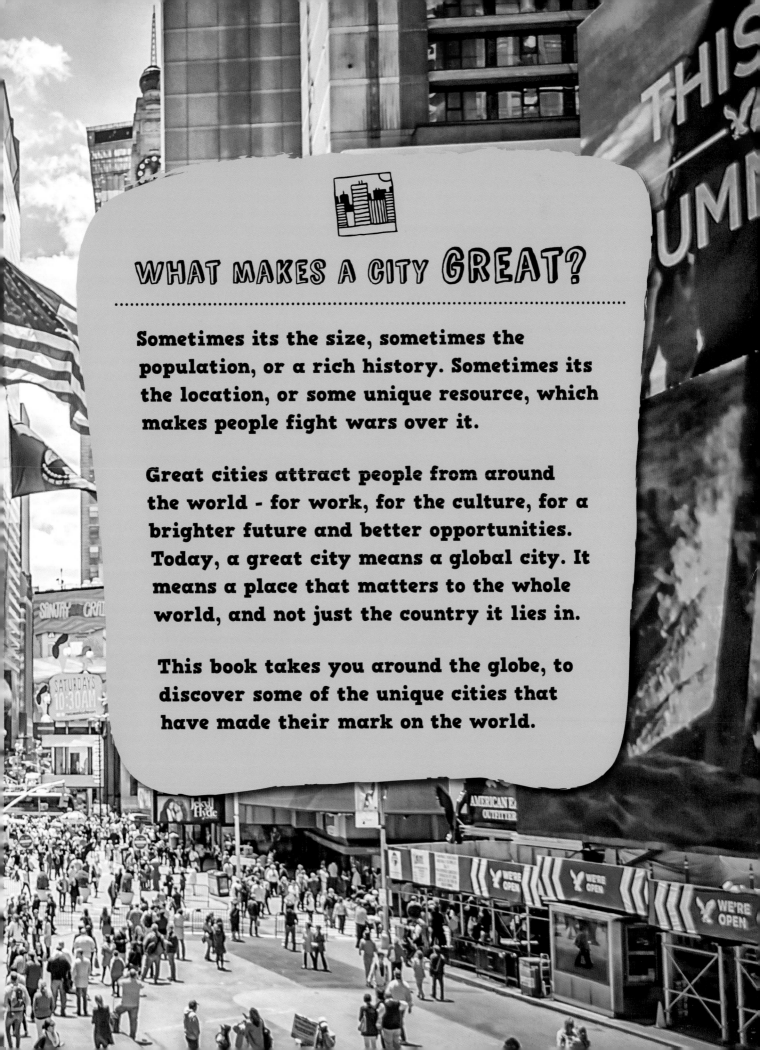

WHAT MAKES A CITY GREAT?

Sometimes its the size, sometimes the population, or a rich history. Sometimes its the location, or some unique resource, which makes people fight wars over it.

Great cities attract people from around the world - for work, for the culture, for a brighter future and better opportunities. Today, a great city means a global city. It means a place that matters to the whole world, and not just the country it lies in.

This book takes you around the globe, to discover some of the unique cities that have made their mark on the world.

OSLO
is the capital of Norway, and one of Europe's fastest-growing capitals. The Nobel Peace Prize is awarded annually in Oslo.

HELSINKI
is the capital and largest city of Finland. 300 islands make up the land area, whereas the rest of the city is actually sea!

COPENHAGEN,
capital of Denmark and second largest city of Scandinavia. Home to designer furniture and Hans Christian Andersen.

ST. PETERSBURG,
known as the City of Palaces, it is Russia's 'window to the West.'

WARSAW,
capital and largest city of Poland. Known for its role in World War II and the 'Warsaw uprising.'

DUBLIN,
capital and largest city of Ireland. Home city of Oscar Wilde, Bernard Shaw and James Joyce. UNESCO City of Literature.

BALTIC SEA

NORTH SEA

ATLANTIC OCEAN

BUDAPEST,
capital of Hungary, and one of the largest cities in the European Union. Known as ''Pearl of the Danube.'

BLACK SEA

MEDITERRANEAN SEA

LISBON,
the capital and largest city of Portugal. Known for its naval glory, Vasco da Gama sailed from here to India.

MUNICH,
capital and largest city of the German state of Bavaria. Played an important role in the World Wars.

NAPLES,
is the largest city in southeast Italy. It's known for its cultural history. And pizza, which was invented here!

DUBROVNIK,
historic walled city in Croatia. Known as 'Pearl of the Adriatic' and a UNESCO World Heritage Site.

Great Cities of

EUROPE

WINDMILLS (*Molen* in Dutch) are icons of Holland, and the Dutch celebrate a 'National Windmill Day'.

BICYCLES are a favourite mode of transport in Amsterdam. There are more than 880,000 bikes in the city!

Amsterdam

Amsterdam began life in the 13th century as a small fishing village on the Amstel river, but it soon developed into a seafaring community with global influence. Today, the capital of Holland is a liberal city steeped in art and culture, and its famous canals have earned it the nickname 'Venice of the North.'

QUICK FACTS

- **Local Name:** Amsterdam
- **Languages:** Dutch, German, French and English
- **CLAIM TO FAME:** Maritime history and great art!

THE GOLDEN AGE (1585-1672)

Amsterdam was the centre of commerce in the 17th century. Within the city, merchants controlled the world's first Stock Exchange, and sent out expeditions to India and other parts of the trading world. Profits made by the Dutch East India Company helped Amsterdam prosper. It was an important time for art too. Artists like Rembrandt and Vermeer painted many portraits and scenes depicting Dutch social life, which are now considered masterpieces.

A coin minted by the Dutch East India Company

Amsterdam Timeline

1270	1380	1602	1808	1889	1928
Dam built on Amstel River	Construction of first canals begins	Stock Exchange and Dutch East India Company founded	Amsterdam becomes capital of Kingdom of Holland	Centraal Station connects Amsterdam to Europe	Amsterdam hosts the Olympics

The **CANAL RING** is now a UNESCO World Heritage site.

VINCENT VAN GOGH (1853 -1890) Amsterdam holds the largest collection of his work.

REMBRANDT VAN RIJN (1606 -1669) 'Dutch Golden Age' painter

JOHANNES VERMEER (1632 -1675) and **JAN STEEN (1626 -1679)** Painted for rich clients in Amsterdam.

BENEDICT DE SPINOZA (1632 -1677) Key philosopher from 'The Enlightenment' movement.

Amsterdam has more than **1200 bridges** on its waterways!

THE CANAL RING

In the 17th century, Amsterdam was transformed into an important port city with the creation of the 'Canal Ring'. Three main canals, *Herengracht, Prinsengracht,* and *Keizersgracht,* were dug in concentric circles to help transport goods in and out of the city, and more canals followed. Soon traders' houses came up on the banks. These 'canal houses' were narrow and tall structures, with basements and attics to store goods. A pulley outside would move the larger cargo out of the boats and into the house.

ANNE FRANK

Anne Frank was a young Jewish girl who lived most of her life in Amsterdam. Born in Germany in 1929, she moved there with her family in 1933. When the Germans occupied the city, her family were forced into hiding for two years. But they were found by Nazi officers and moved to concentration camps. Anne died of an illness in 1945, a few months before her 16th birthday. Her diary was later found by her father, and published in 1947. **The Diary of Anne Frank** has since become one of the most inspiring books ever published.

The **BLOEMENMARKT** is the world's only floating flower market, and has been open since 1862!

1940 - 1945 German occupation of Amsterdam

1975 Amsterdam gets a new flag

1977 Amsterdam Metro begins service

Athens

Athens is the capital and the largest city of Greece. But really it is famous for being one of the oldest and most important cities in the world. It is often called the 'Cradle of Civilization' because of its role in the shaping of western philosophy, politics, arts and sciences.

QUICK FACTS

- **Local Name:** Athens, Athina
- **Languages:** Mainly Greek and its dialects, and English
- **CLAIM TO FAME:** Cradle of Western Civilisation!

THE GREATEST IDEA EVER!

Democracy, a form of government where all citizens can participate equally in the creation of laws, was born in Athens. The word itself derives from Greek, and means 'rule of the people'. The Athenians had a 'direct democracy', where 500 citizens were chosen to serve for a year and make the laws. The rest of the citizens would vote on whether to enact them. (Although 'all citizens' just meant free men - slaves, children and women were not allowed to vote).

What we have in most countries today, is a 'representative democracy'. People vote for their favourite candidates, who will form a government to both make and enact the laws.

THE FIRST CITIZEN OF ATHENS

Pericles (c. 495 – 429 BC) was the most prominent Greek statesman, orator, and general of Athens. Under his rule, Athens reached its golden age. Great writers, thinkers and artists came to the city and flourished here. Pericles also started a project where the city's acropolis ('upper city') was built up with monuments. Many of these survive today, including the famous Parthenon. Pericles also fostered Athenian democracy, and we still use principles from this system today.

Greek mythology says that the Goddess Athena first gave the **Olive Tree** to Athens. The olive is sacred to the Greeks.

Athens Timeline

750-500 BC
City-states like Athens flourish

432 BC
Parthenon is completed

145 BC
Greece becomes part of the Roman empire

1453 AD
Ottoman Turks conquer Greece. Athens' power declines

1833 Athens becomes capital of Greece

1896 First modern Olympic Games held in Athens

1981 Greece becomes member of the European Community

2004
Second Athens Olympic Games are held

The city's most famous building is the **PARTHENON,** which stands on a rocky hill called the Acropolis. Parts of it were designed by Phidias, a famous sculptor, painter and architect.

The **ELGIN MARBLES** or the Parthenon Marbles, were taken from the Parthenon in 1802 by Lord Elgin. These sculptures are now displayed in the British Museum in London.

FAMOUS ATHENIANS

SOCRATES (470-399 BC) Classical Greek philosopher.

PLATO (428-348 BC) was both a philosopher and mathematician.

HERODOTUS (484-425 BC) `Father of History', lived and wrote in Athens

MELINA MERCOURI (1920 – 1994) Actress, singer and politician. She campaigned for the Elgin marbles to be returned to Athens.

NANA MOUSKOURI (b- 1934) renowned singer

ATHENA is the goddess of war, intelligence, skill, reason, art and literature. She is the daughter of Zeus, and the protector of Athens.

The **Theatre of Dionysus** is the oldest surviving theatre in Athens. It was dedicated to Dionysus, the god of wine and patron of drama.

IT ALL STARTED HERE!

Ancient Athens was a great centre of learning. Every subject, from mathematics, science and philosophy, to literature, politics, and the arts, was encouraged here. We owe most of our cultural ideas to the Ancient Greeks. **Theatre** is supposed to have started in Athens, with *tragedies* and *comedies* being staged at the many venues in the city. There were **gymnasiums** everywhere, where people could exercise, bathe and even have philosophical debates. The Greeks were obsessed with sports: they were the ones who started the Olympics!

Barcelona

Barcelona was founded in the 3rd century BC. Later it was occupied by the Romans, Goths, Moors and the Franks, one after the other. Barcelona is located on the Mediterranean coast, and in the Middle Ages it was a major trading port. Today it is Spain's second biggest city, and a major economic hub.

QUICK FACTS

- **Local Name:** Barcelona, Ciutat Comtal *(City of Counts)*
- **Languages:** Catalan and Spanish
- **CLAIM TO FAME:** Gaudí's buildings

PROUD CATALANS

Barcelona is the capital of Catalunya, a region with a rich history and a unique culture. It is also one of Spain's most wealthy and modernised regions. Catalans are proud people, and many think that they are quite separate from the rest of Spain. In fact, Catalunya now has its own parliament. The local language here is Catalan, which is related to Spanish, as well as French and Italian.

Barcelonians do a special regional dance, called the **Sardana.**

Some people say Barcelona was founded by a Carthiginian named **Hamilcar Barca.** Others believe it was the mythical hero **Hercules.**

Gaudí's mosaic salamander, *(el drac, the dragon)* sits in **PARK GÜELL,** and is a popular symbol of Barcelona.

La Mercè is the most important festival in Barcelona, held in honour of the patron saint The Virgin de La Merce. Papier maché figures known as *gegants* are paraded through the city, and people build a *Castell* (a human tower built traditionally in festivals).

BARCELONA TIMELINE

250BC
Founded by Hamilcar Barca

27BC
Roman occupation of 'Barcino'

1000-1200
Barcelona becomes an important port

1640
Catalan revolt against Spanish monarchy

1808
Napolean's forces capture Barcelona

1848
First Spanish railway constructed in Barcelona

1868
Spanish Revolution

1936
Start of the Spanish Civil War

1992
Barcelona hosts the Olympics

The **BASILICA OF THE SAGRADA FAMILIA (the Holy Family)** was begun in 1882. Gaudí took over in 1883, and it will be completed around 2028. The church has taken longer to build than the **Great Pyramids**, which took only 20 years!

FAMOUS BARCELONIANS

JOAN MIRÓ (1893-1983)
Surrealist painter and sculptor

PABLO PICASSO (1881-1973) and **SALVADOR DALI (1904-1989)**
Their work was exhibited widely in Barcelona.

JOSÉ CARRERAS (b-1946)
Prominent opera tenor

CASA MILÀ is part of the UNESCO World Heritage sites designed by Gaudí.

THE CITY OF GAUDÍ

Antoni Gaudí (1852-1926) was a Spanish architect. His style was called 'Modernista'. His work was very much influenced by nature and religion. Many of his buildings are in Barcelona, including the most famous one, *the Sagrada Familia*.

Berlin

The capital and largest city of Germany, Berlin is the second most populous in Europe, after London. It lies in north-east Germany and is also one of its 16 Länder (states). It has a long history, and is known today for its high-tech industry.

QUICK FACTS

- **Local Name:** Berlin
- **Languages:** German
- **CLAIM TO FAME:** Historic capital and World War II history

Berlin probably gets its name from the German word for bear, *Bär,* which also appears on its coat of arms.

THE WALL

After World War II, Berlin was divided into several zones, the east occupied by the Soviet Union, and the west by the Allied powers. In 1961, the government of East Berlin decided to build a wall, to stop people escaping to the west. This was during the Cold War, when the democratic Western world and the communist East did not get along.

By 1987, the Soviet Union was collapsing, and their control on East Germany weakening. In 1989, the borders were opened and people celebrated by tearing down the Berlin Wall. Germany was reunified as a single country in 1990.

The **Berlin Wall** was a symbol of the 'Iron Curtain,' which separated Western and Eastern Europe for many years. Today, its eastern side is an open art gallery for artists and graffitists!

Berlin Timeline

1163	Berlin founded by 'Albert the Bear'
1810	University of Berlin established
1933	Reichstag Fire
1940	Bombing of Berlin in World War II
1945	Battle of Berlin begins
1945	Death of Adolf Hitler in the Führerbunker
1990	German reunification, Berlin made capital of the Federal Republic of Germany

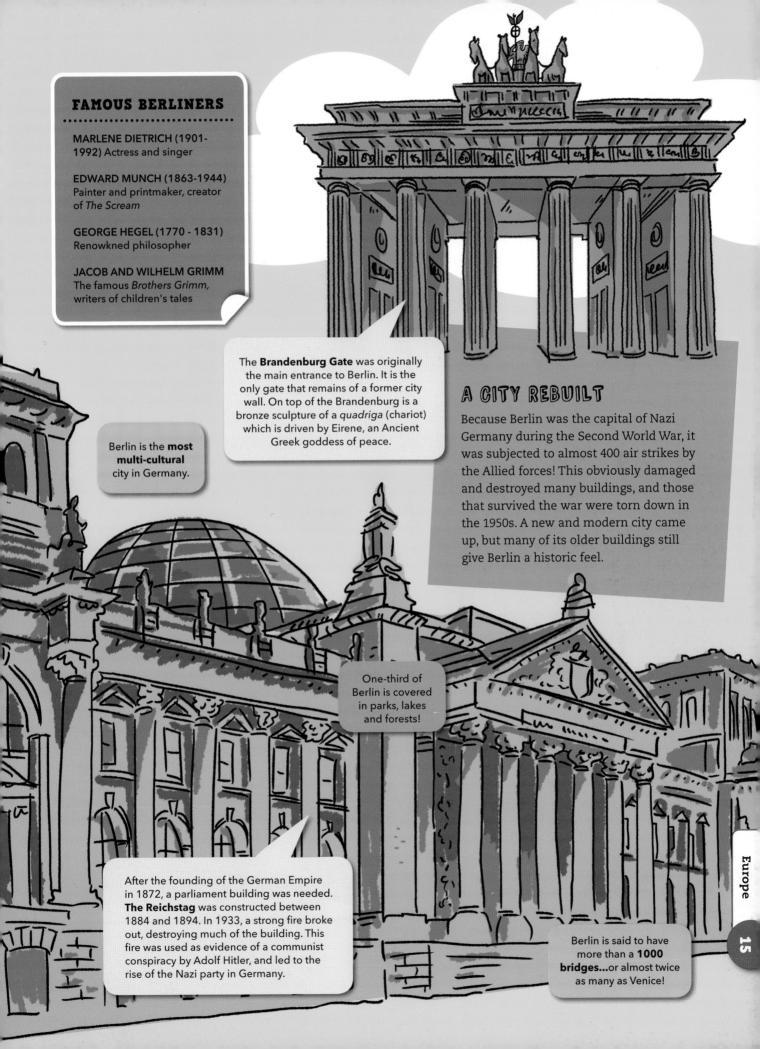

FAMOUS BERLINERS

MARLENE DIETRICH (1901-1992) Actress and singer

EDWARD MUNCH (1863-1944) Painter and printmaker, creator of *The Scream*

GEORGE HEGEL (1770 - 1831) Renowkned philosopher

JACOB AND WILHELM GRIMM The famous *Brothers Grimm,* writers of children's tales

The **Brandenburg Gate** was originally the main entrance to Berlin. It is the only gate that remains of a former city wall. On top of the Brandenburg is a bronze sculpture of a *quadriga* (chariot) which is driven by Eirene, an Ancient Greek goddess of peace.

Berlin is the **most multi-cultural** city in Germany.

A CITY REBUILT

Because Berlin was the capital of Nazi Germany during the Second World War, it was subjected to almost 400 air strikes by the Allied forces! This obviously damaged and destroyed many buildings, and those that survived the war were torn down in the 1950s. A new and modern city came up, but many of its older buildings still give Berlin a historic feel.

One-third of Berlin is covered in parks, lakes and forests!

After the founding of the German Empire in 1872, a parliament building was needed. **The Reichstag** was constructed between 1884 and 1894. In 1933, a strong fire broke out, destroying much of the building. This fire was used as evidence of a communist conspiracy by Adolf Hitler, and led to the rise of the Nazi party in Germany.

Berlin is said to have more than a **1000 bridges...**or almost twice as many as Venice!

Brussels

Brussels in Belgium's largest city and its capital. From a small marshy town in the 6th century, it has grown into a truly international city today. More than 25% of its inhabitants come from outside Belgium. It is also a bilingual city, with people speaking both Flemish (Belgian Dutch) and French.

QUICK FACTS

- **Local Name:** Bruxelles, Brussel
- **Languages:** Dutch/ Flemish, French and English
- **CLAIM TO FAME:** Capital of the European Union

ONE CITY, MANY RULERS

In the 6th century, Brussels was just a small settlement on the marshes of the river Senne. Over the next 500 years it evolved into a fortified town. In the 12th century was ruled by the **Dukes of Brabant**. Between the 15th and the 17th centuries, it was the **Dukes of Burgundy**, and then the Spanish and the Austrian **Hapsburgs** took over. The **French** threw out the Austrians, but Napolean was in turn defeated at Waterloo in 1815 by the allied European armies. Belgium was then joined with **Holland**. Following a revolt against the Dutch in 1830, Brussels finally became the capital of a new **Kingdom of Belgium**.

Tintin and Snowy, depicted in graffitti on a building in Brussels.

THE ADVENTURES OF TINTIN

The world-famous **Tintin,** and his trusty dog Snowy, were the creations of cartoonist Georges Prosper Remi (1907–1983), who wrote under the pen name **Hergé**.

He began his career by drawing for the journal *Le Boy-Scout Belge*, and later moved on to comic books. He created many different characters, but the Tintin series proved to be one of the most popular European comics of the 20th century.

Brussels Timeline

580
Brussels is founded as a marshy settlement village

1010
Fortified walls are built

1200s
Brussels becomes an important trade hub

1402-1452
The Town Hall is constructed

1831
Belgian king Leopold II ascends the throne to the independent kingdom

1944-45
Nazi forces bombard the city

2000
Brussels is European City of Culture

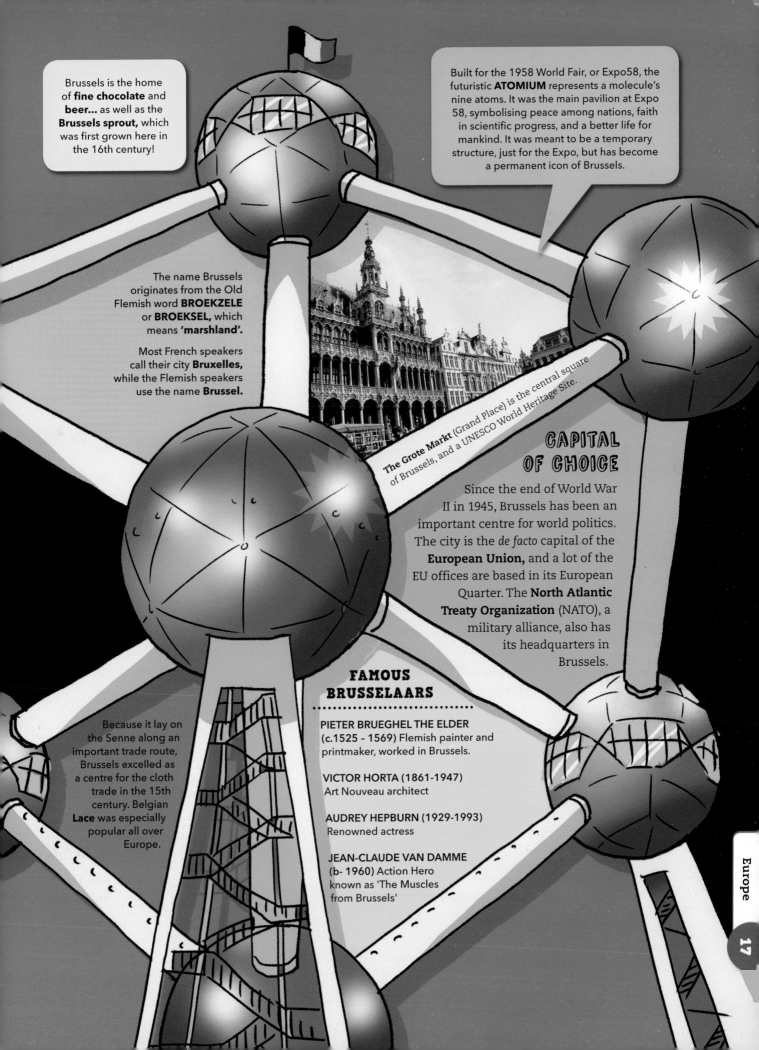

Brussels is the home of **fine chocolate** and **beer...** as well as the **Brussels sprout,** which was first grown here in the 16th century!

Built for the 1958 World Fair, or Expo58, the futuristic **ATOMIUM** represents a molecule's nine atoms. It was the main pavilion at Expo 58, symbolising peace among nations, faith in scientific progress, and a better life for mankind. It was meant to be a temporary structure, just for the Expo, but has become a permanent icon of Brussels.

The name Brussels originates from the Old Flemish word **BROEKZELE** or **BROEKSEL,** which means **'marshland'.**

Most French speakers call their city **Bruxelles,** while the Flemish speakers use the name **Brussel.**

The Grote Markt (Grand Place) is the central square of Brussels, and a UNESCO World Heritage Site.

CAPITAL OF CHOICE

Since the end of World War II in 1945, Brussels has been an important centre for world politics. The city is the *de facto* capital of the **European Union,** and a lot of the EU offices are based in its European Quarter. The **North Atlantic Treaty Organization** (NATO), a military alliance, also has its headquarters in Brussels.

FAMOUS BRUSSELAARS

PIETER BRUEGHEL THE ELDER (c.1525 – 1569) Flemish painter and printmaker, worked in Brussels.

VICTOR HORTA (1861-1947) Art Nouveau architect

AUDREY HEPBURN (1929-1993) Renowned actress

JEAN-CLAUDE VAN DAMME (b- 1960) Action Hero known as 'The Muscles from Brussels'

Because it lay on the Senne along an important trade route, Brussels excelled as a centre for the cloth trade in the 15th century. Belgian **Lace** was especially popular all over Europe.

Glasgow

Glasgow started off in the 6th century as a small village on the river Clyde. It was the seat of a bishopric, and soon became a 'royal burgh'. It grew into one of the most important and prosperous trading ports of the 18th century. Today it is the biggest city in Scotland.

QUICK FACTS

- **Local Name:** Glaschu, Glesga
- **Languages:** English, Scots, Scottish, Gaelic
- **CLAIM TO FAME:** Shipbuilding heritage

The name 'Glasgow' comes from a Gaelic phrase meaning 'green valley' or 'dear green place'.

The futuristic **Riverside Museum,** was designed by acclaimed architect Zaha Hadid, and opened in 2011.

The Clyde Auditorium, (or **The Armadillo**), is a concert venue on the Clyde. Its design was inspired by ship hulls.

CLYDEBUILT

Glasgow has a rich history as a shipbuilding city. In the 18th century, a lot of the tobacco trade between America and Europe passed through Glasgow. This made the city quite affluent. After the tobacco trade declined, it was replaced by textiles, coal, steel and shipbuilding.

Ships built on the Clydeside included the **Cutty Sark** and **HMS Hood,** and were exported all over the world because of their quality. Shipyards attracted labourers by the thousands and the town grew.

Glasgow was then called the second city of the empire, after London. But the prosperity came at a price, and the German *Luftwaffe* (air force) bombed Clydeside quite extensively during World War II.

GLASGOW STYLE

CHARLES RENNIE MACKINTOSH was a talented designer, artist and architect. He was born in Glasgow in 1868 and studied at the Glasgow School of Art. His unique Art Nouveau designs are considered central to what is now known as the **Glasgow Style**. Although he worked in the city for 20 years, he was better appreciated in Europe. He moved to London in his later years, but when his work gained recognition after his death in 1928, he was often referred to as the father of the Glasgow Style.

A lithograph poster by Mackintosh for **The Scottish Musical Review**, 1896.

FAMOUS GLASWEGIANS

JOHN LOGIE BAIRD (1888-1946) Inventor of television

GORDON BROWN (b-1951) Former UK Prime Minister UK

SIR ALEX FERGUSON (b-1941) Legendary football manager

ANDY MURRAY (b-1987) Tennis player and Wimbledon Champion.

The term **'Glaswegian'** was introduced in 1817 by Sir Walter Scott, in his novel *Rob Roy*.

The **Hydro** is an multi-use arena, which hosted several events of the Commonwealth Games in 2014.

Glasgow Timeline

6th century
St Mungo builds a church at *Glas Gu*

1286
Glasgow Bridge built over the Clyde

1451
Glasgow University is founded

1492
Glasgow is given an archbishop

1814
Glasgow Green becomes Europe's first public park

1990
Glasgow is made European City of Culture

2014
Glasgow hosts the Commonwealth Games

1674
The first cargo of tobacco arrives

(poster text) THE SCOTTISH MUSICAL REVIEW PUBLISHED & THE 1ST OF EACH MONTH PRICE TWO PENCE

Istanbul

This ancient city sits on both sides of the Bosphorus strait. Once known as the mighty Constantinople, it was home to two of the world's great empires. Traditional and yet very modern, Istanbul today is a rising power and the largest city of Turkey.

QUICK FACTS

- **Local Name:** Istanbul
- **Languages:** Turkish, English
- **CLAIM TO FAME:** Unique geography, and great empires!

The Hagia Sophia, or *Aya Sofia*, was the cathedral of Constantinople, built by Constantine the Great in 537 AD. It contained many important Christian relics. When the Ottomans took over, they found the church so beautiful that they converted it into the Imperial Mosque, instead of breaking it down. It was redecorated in Islamic style, but the original mosaics were retained. Nowadays the Hagia Sophia is a very popular museum.

Istanbul is the world's only metropolis to extend into **more than one continent!**

THE GRANDEST OF HISTORIES

Istanbul has been inhabited since 3000 BC, but it became a city under the Greeks in the 7th century BC. Their King, Byzas, named it **Byzantium.**

When the Roman emperor Constantine took over in 300 AD, he decided to rebuild the whole city. In 330, he declared the city the capital of the entire Roman Empire, and renamed it **Constantinople.** Under his rule, the city really prospered. Between 395 and 1453, the rivalry between the Byzantines and the Ottoman Turks led to the city's decline.

The next big change came with the Ottoman conquest in 1453, under Sultan Mehmet II. The Ottoman Empire ruled the city until 1922, and renamed it **Istanbul.**

Turkey was occupied by the Allied forces during World War I, and in 1923 the War of Independence took place. Istanbul became part of the Republic of Turkey, although the capital was moved to Ankara. Istanbul prospered again in the 1970s, and grew into a modern metropolis.

Tulips were first grown in Istanbul under Ottoman rule. They were exported to Holland, and Europe, from here.

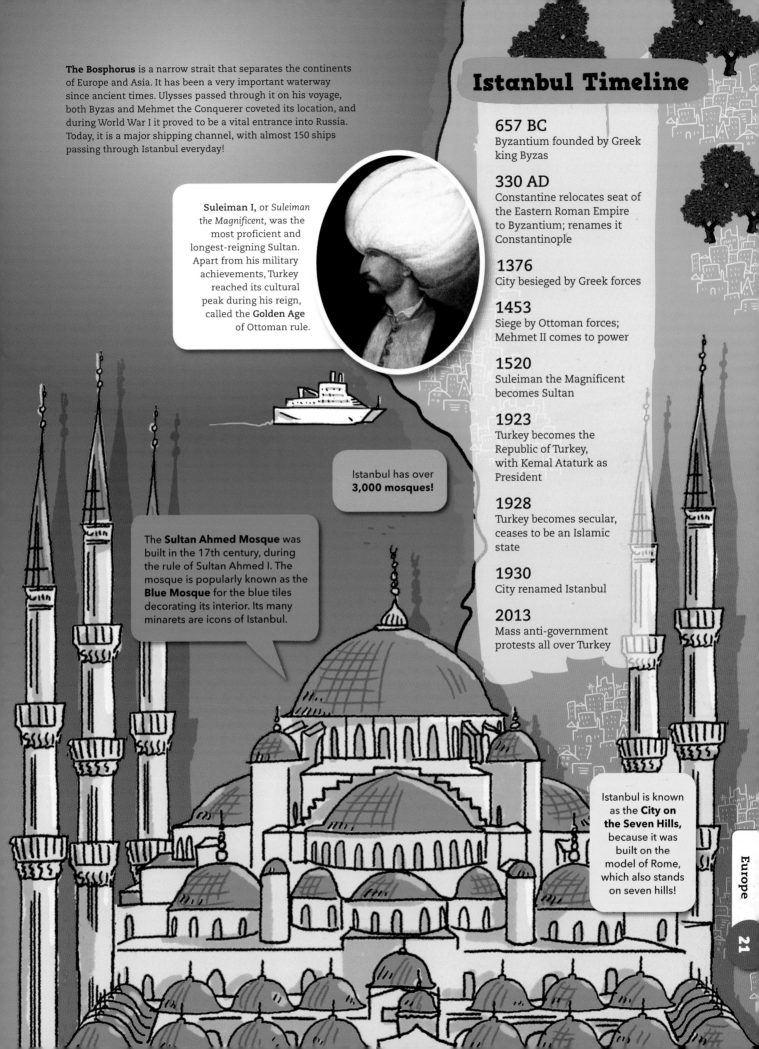

The Bosphorus is a narrow strait that separates the continents of Europe and Asia. It has been a very important waterway since ancient times. Ulysses passed through it on his voyage, both Byzas and Mehmet the Conquerer coveted its location, and during World War I it proved to be a vital entrance into Russia. Today, it is a major shipping channel, with almost 150 ships passing through Istanbul everyday!

Suleiman I, or *Suleiman the Magnificent,* was the most proficient and longest-reigning Sultan. Apart from his military achievements, Turkey reached its cultural peak during his reign, called the **Golden Age** of Ottoman rule.

Istanbul Timeline

657 BC
Byzantium founded by Greek king Byzas

330 AD
Constantine relocates seat of the Eastern Roman Empire to Byzantium; renames it Constantinople

1376
City besieged by Greek forces

1453
Siege by Ottoman forces; Mehmet II comes to power

1520
Suleiman the Magnificent becomes Sultan

1923
Turkey becomes the Republic of Turkey, with Kemal Ataturk as President

1928
Turkey becomes secular, ceases to be an Islamic state

1930
City renamed Istanbul

2013
Mass anti-government protests all over Turkey

Istanbul has over **3,000 mosques!**

The **Sultan Ahmed Mosque** was built in the 17th century, during the rule of Sultan Ahmed I. The mosque is popularly known as the **Blue Mosque** for the blue tiles decorating its interior. Its many minarets are icons of Istanbul.

Istanbul is known as the **City on the Seven Hills,** because it was built on the model of Rome, which also stands on seven hills!

London

London is the capital of the United Kingdom. It is one of the oldest of the world's great cities, dating back almost 2000 years. London is Britain's largest metropolis, its economic and cultural centre, and its most cosmopolitan city.

Francis Drake's ship, the **Golden Hinde.**

THE ROMANS

The Romans invaded Britain in 43 AD. They thought the river Thames was an ideal place to build a port, and founded the town of **Londinium** on its banks around 50 AD. Like Rome itself it had a forum and an amphitheatre, where gladiators fought. Luxury goods were imported for the rich, including wine, glass, silks and ivory.

In 61 AD, Queen Boudicca of the Iceni tribe, from the east of England, led a rebellion. Her army burned the city down, but was defeated by the Romans. Londinium was rebuilt, and thrived again, becoming the biggest city in Britannia (the Roman name for Britain).

An Anglo-Saxon helmet, found at Sutton Hoo in southern England.

THE ANGLO-SAXONS

The Romans left around 410 AD, and Britain was invaded by the Anglo-Saxon tribes from Scandinavia and Germany. They ruled for about 500 years. London declined in this time, although it was still a valuable port. The Danes raided and conquered London, and other parts of England, around 840 AD. The Anglo-Saxon king **Alfred the Great,** defeated the Danes in 878, and repaired London's Roman walls.

In 1042, Edward the Confessor built a wooden palace at Westminster, which became the seat of government. He also built the Westminster Abbey.

THE TUDORS (1485 - 1603)

The Tudors were a Welsh-English family. The most famous Tudor figures include **Henry VIII,** and his six wives. He had two of them beheaded at the Tower of London! Henry also founded the Church of England, simply because he wanted a divorce from his first wife in 1534 and the Catholic Church didn't allow it.

The other famous Tudor monarch was **Elizabeth I,** whose rule is remembered as England's Golden Age. Trade, exploration, literature, and the arts prospered during her reign. Explorer Walter Raleigh helped colonise America. And Francis Drake became the first Englishman to sail around the world in his ship, The Golden Hinde.

MEDIEVAL LONDON

William the Conqueror was crowned king in 1066, and London was ruled by the Normans. William is credited with building a stone tower, which would later become the **Tower of London.** In 1087 a new cathedral, **St. Pauls**, was built. A stone bridge was built across the Thames in 1176. London was a busy town: there was trading, sports, racing, dancing, wrestling, skating on ice, and all sorts of activities, to keep its large population busy. There were also famines and plagues, including the Black Death, which claimed half of London - almost 40,000 people!

Queen Boudicca burnt down London, but she has her own monument in the city!

The Great Fire of London, 1666, painted by an anonymous artist.

THE VICTORIANS (1837-1901)

London was now the largest city in the world, with over 1 million people. Many of its icons, like Trafalgar Square, the Houses of Parliament and the Underground Tube, were built in the 19th century. **The Great Exhibition** was held in 1851, showing the latest technology to the world. Victorian London was also famous for some terrible things, like the thick and green pea-souper Fog, which often covered the city. Or Jack the Ripper, a murderer who was never caught. **Charles Dickens** famously brought this era to life in his books.

LONDON IN THE WAR

London was doing very well in the early 20th century. It became a manufacturing town, with busy mills and factories, breweries and shipyards. Trade was booming. But during World War II (1939-1945), the city really suffered. Air and missile attacks during the **Blitz** killed nearly 25,000 people. Londoners had to sleep in Underground stations, or in bunkers. Many areas were destroyed. After the war ended, Londoners recovered quickly, rebuilding the city and its economy. Immigrants from British colonies arrived here, and Britain joined the **European Community.** The population grew rapidly and the city was modernized.

THE STUARTS (1603-1714)

The Stuart rule in London witnessed the **Gunpowder Plot,** the infamous attempt to kill James I. Guy Fawkes was one of the conspirators, who decided to blow up the Parliament in 1605. He was arrested before he could do any damage.

In 1665, **The Plague** returned to London, like it had many times before. But this time, nearly 70,000 Londoners perished!

Then came the **Great Fire** of 1666, which started at a bakery in Pudding Lane. The fire raged for five days, burning down a large part of London, including St Paul's Cathedral. The silver lining to this tragedy was that London was soon rebuilt, with fresh ideas.

THE GEORGIANS (1714-1830)

Georgian London saw rapid growth and a revival in architecture. Many famous landmarks of today came up during this time. **Buckingham Palace** was built in 1703, and the **British Museum** was founded in 1753. The iconic **St Paul's** cathedral, designed by Christopher Wren, was completed in 1708. London spread to new districts, in the West end and across the Thames in South London. The printing press came to Fleet Street .

QUICK FACTS

- **Local Name:** London
- **Languages:** English, and many other languages
- **CLAIM TO FAME:** A great mix of past, present and future!

London Timeline

50 AD
The Romans found Londonium

c. 180 Stone walls are built around London

c. 650 London flourishes under the Saxons

1348-49 Black Death strikes the city

1666 The Great Fire of London

1839 Trafalgar Square is created

1881 Natural History Museum is founded

1903 First council houses are built in city

1960s End of British Empire, the docks decline

2000 London Eye opens to public

2005 Tube and bus bombings

2012 London hosts the Olympics

LIQUID HISTORY

The Thames is London's lifeline. 30 million years ago, it was part of the German river Rhine, when Britain was not yet an island. It came to be in its current form and shape some 3,000 years ago. Archaeologists have found settlements along the river that are 40,000 years old!

London was first a port, then a great city later, and the river served everyone from the Romans to the Victorians. The river can boast royal palaces at Hampton Court, Kew, Whitehall and Richmond. Festivals like the Lord Mayor's pageant, the Doggett's race in honour of watermen, and the race between the Universities of Oxford and Cambridge, started hundreds of years ago and still continue. During World War II, the London docks were bombed and seriously damaged.

Nowadays, the Thames within London is not used for trade, but the riverside is a leisure and luxury destination instead.

MODERN LONDON

Today London is a cosmopolitan city. It is much more multicultural and globally connected than the rest of the UK. At the cutting edge of finance, art, design and architecture, London is a world capital city.

The award-winning 30 St Mary Axe, was designed by architects Foster and Partners in 2004. It is better known as **THE GHERKIN.**

THE SHARD was designed by Renzo Piano, and at 310 meters (1016 ft) it was (briefly!) Europe's tallest skyscraper when finished in 2012.

THE LONDON EYE was only meant to be a temporary structure, built for the Millenium celebrations in 2000. It proved so popular that now its a permanent part of the skyline!

Structures like the **Orbit,** and the **Velodrome** were built for the 2012 Olympics, and are part of a rich and quirky architectural legacy.

WILLIAM SHAKESPEARE (1564-1616) Poet and playwright, often called the greatest writer in the English language

SAMUEL PEPYS (1633-1703) Member of Parliament, most famous for the Diary he wrote about London

EDMOND HALLEY (1656-1742) Astronomer and mathematician, credited with discovering the comet named after him.

HENRY PURCELL (1659-1695) One of the greatest composers of *English Baroque* music

LORD BYRON (1788-1824) politician, and one of the greatest British poets, leader of the *Romantic* movement in poetry

CHARLES BABBAGE (1791-1891) Inventor and engineer, who devised the first mechanical 'computer'

BEATRIX POTTER (1866-1943) Children's author and illustrator, creator of Peter Rabbit

CHARLIE CHAPLIN (1889-1977) Silent era actor and comedian, known for his *'Tramp'* persona

ENID BLYTON (1897-1968) Children's author, creator of *Noddy* and *Famous Five*

ALAN TURING (1912-1954) Mathematician and scientist, he played a vital role in decoding German messages during World War II

DAVID BECKHAM (B-1975) Footballer for England, Manchester United and Real Madrid

Madrid

Madrid is the capital of Spain. In the 9th century, Muslim rulers built a fort on the river Manzanares, (which they called al-Majrit). This became Madrid, today the third largest city in Europe, after London and Berlin.

QUICK FACTS

- **Local Name:** Madrid
- **Languages:** Spanish
- **CLAIM TO FAME:** Bullfights and Flamenco!

Madrid is located on a plateau 650 metres above sea level. It is the **highest capital city** in Europe.

THE PALACIO REAL DE MADRID (Madrid Royal Palace) stands on the original site of the 9th-century fort *Al-Majrit*.

A ROYAL HISTORY

Madrid has been inhabited for thousands of years. It became notable in the 9th century when Arab rulers, the **Moors,** built a fort here. Around 923 AD, Christian forces under King Leon tried to 'reconquer' Madrid from the Muslims. It was eventually brought under Christian rule in 1083. Madrid grew in importance over the years, and in 1561, it was made the capital of Spain.

The Spanish Hapsburgs took over in the 17th century, and the city really flourished. This was Madrid's Golden Age – art, architecture and the economy soared. French rule came in the 18th century, until the Spaniards won the War of Independence in 1814. King Fernando, who had been imprisoned by Napolean, returned to rule and redevelop Madrid.

Madrid Timeline

9th Century
Mehmed I constructs palace at the site of the present-day Palacio Real

1808
Napoleon's troops invade Madrid

1085
Alfonso VI conquers the citadel near the river Majrit, from which Madrid gets its name.

1814
War of Independence

1561
Philip II moves the capital from Toledo to Madrid

1939
Madrid is taken over by the Nationalists

1716-1788
Carlos III modernises Madrid

2004
Terrorist bombs on several trains during the rush hours kill 191 people

FAMOUS MADRILEÑOS

PENÉLOPE CRUZ (b-1974)
Academy award-winning actress

PLÁCIDO DOMINGO (b-1941)
International tenor and conductor

FRANCISCO GOYA (1746-1828)
Madrid-based court painter

MARIO VARGAS LLOSA (b-1936)
Peruvian-Spanish writer, 2010 Nobel laureate in Literature.

BULLFIGHTING is quite popular in Madrid. The most famous bullring in the city is called *Plaza de Torros de Las Ventas.*

The city of Madrid is sometimes referred to as **Los Madriles.**

THE SPANISH CIVIL WAR

In 1932, Spain became a Republic. The Catholic Church, the military, and supporters of fascism wanted the monarchy to return. This group was called the Nationalists. Their opponents were the Leftist parties. A civil war broke out between the two groups in 1936 and the Nationalists, led by General Franco, won. Madrid suffered a lot of damage but survived as the capital. Spain was declared a monarchy, but Franco ruled the country as a dictator until his death in 1975.

The famous music and dance form of **FLAMENCO** comes from Madrid.

Moscow

Moscow is the capital and the largest city of Russia. It is also the country's cultural and industrial hub. It is Russia's most populous city, and is named after the river that runs through it: the Moskva.

RED SQUARE

The **Red Square** is a famous public square in Moscow, and contains many important buildings and monuments. On one end of Red Square stands the **Moscow Kremlin** (fort), which dates from 1156. It has been witness to every major political event in Russia. **Saint Basil the Blessed,** on the other side of the square, is a beautiful Russian Orthodox Church.

The name Red Square has nothing to do with its red bricks, or Communism. It comes from the Russian word *krasnaya*, which can either mean 'beautiful' or 'red.' It first referred to St. Basil's church, and later to the entire square.

Moscow is one of the **MOST EXPENSIVE** cities in the world.

For 600 years, Moscow, and St Basil's, has been the spiritual centre of **Orthodox Christianity.**

Moscow is one of the **COLDEST** cities in the world too!

QUICK FACTS

- **Local Name:** Moskva
- **Languages:** Russian
- **CLAIM TO FAME:** Influential history, Home of the Orthodox Church

IVAN THE TERRIBLE

Ivan IV Vasilyevich (1533-1584), was the first 'Czar' of all Russia. He was a devout Christian, and took the title 'Czar' from 'Caesar'. Ivan became ruler at the young age of 3, when his father died. He was a very intelligent man, but had a bad temper. He is said to have killed his own son, and blinded the architect of St. Basil's Cathedral. He acquired vast lands through ruthless means, and created a central government in Moscow. He also created the *Oprichniki*, the first secret police force. When Ivan died, Russia was left in a state of ruin.

Ivan's name does not mean 'terrible' at all! It actually means 'awesome' or 'formidable' in Russian.

The historic **Kremlin Clock,** on the Spasskaya Tower of the Kremlin, chimes on the quarter hour, and also plays music.

CITY OF LETTERS

Russian literature is famous all over the world, and Moscow was where many great authors penned their works. **Leo Tolstoy,** author of *War and Peace* and *Anna Karenina*, had a winter home in Moscow. **Alexander Pushkin,** was born in Moscow and lived here for many years. **Anton Chekhov,** known for his plays and short stories, spent his youth here, struggling for work and writing. **Fyodor Dostoyevsky** was born here. **Maxim Gorky** and **Nikolai Gogol** both lived and worked in Moscow. There was hardly a famous figure in literature who didn't have some connection with the city.

Moscow Timeline

1147
Prince Yuri Dolgoruky founds the city of Moscow

1752
A devastating fire destroys one-third of Moscow

1812
Napoleonic Wars

1877
Tchaikovsky's ballet "Swan Lake" premières at the Bolshoi Theatre

1918
Moscow becomes the capital of Russia again after 215 years

1941
WWII: Operation Typhoon, Germany begins an offensive against Moscow

1991
Soviet Union ceases to exist

2002
150 hostages die in the Moscow Theatre Siege

Paris

Paris has been the capital of France since 508 AD. It became a continental leader in art and education during the 11th century. It was Europe's largest city up until the 18th century, and today it is one of the world's foremost cities for art, fashion and commerce.

QUICK FACTS

- **Local Name:** Paris
- **Languages:** French
- **CLAIM TO FAME:** Intellectual city, with an eye for fashion!

Paris is often called **"La Ville-Lumière"** (The City of Light).

CITY OF CULTURE

Paris has always been a very creative city. Some of the world's best artists, authors and poets have found inspiration here. The city's intellectual **Left Bank** (*Rive Gauche*) was home to countless writers, including George Orwell, Jean-Paul Sartre, Ernest Hemingway and Baudelaire. They mixed with famous artists like Pablo Picasso and Henri Matisse. Today Paris thrives on its artistic vibe.

The *Sacré-Cœur* basilica sits atop the **MONTMARTRE,** and is the highest point in the city. Montmartre was once a very artistic area, and painters such as **Claude Monet, Salvador Dalí,** and **Vincent van Gogh** worked in studios here.

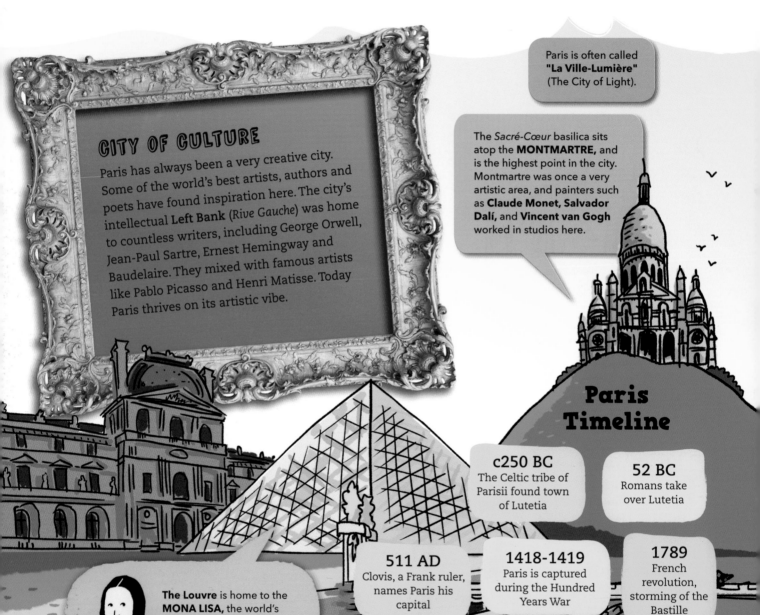

Paris Timeline

c250 BC
The Celtic tribe of Parisii found town of Lutetia

52 BC
Romans take over Lutetia

511 AD
Clovis, a Frank ruler, names Paris his capital

1418-1419
Paris is captured during the Hundred Years War

1789
French revolution, storming of the Bastille

1944
Liberation of Paris in World War II

1994
Eurostar railway between Paris and London begins

1997
Diana, Princess of Wales, dies in an automobile accident in Paris

The Louvre is home to the **MONA LISA,** the world's most famous painting. It was painted by the great **Leonardo da Vinci** in 1503, and is the portrait of Lisa Gherardini, wife of a Florentine merchant.

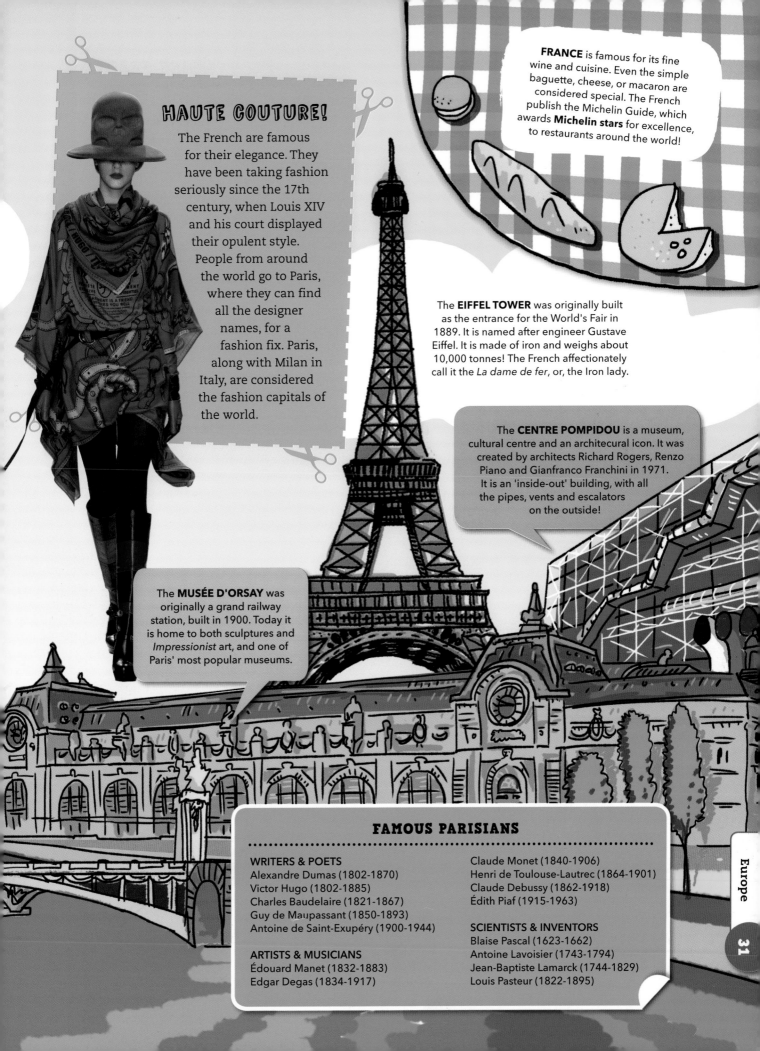

HAUTE COUTURE!

The French are famous for their elegance. They have been taking fashion seriously since the 17th century, when Louis XIV and his court displayed their opulent style. People from around the world go to Paris, where they can find all the designer names, for a fashion fix. Paris, along with Milan in Italy, are considered the fashion capitals of the world.

FRANCE is famous for its fine wine and cuisine. Even the simple baguette, cheese, or macaron are considered special. The French publish the Michelin Guide, which awards **Michelin stars** for excellence, to restaurants around the world!

The **EIFFEL TOWER** was originally built as the entrance for the World's Fair in 1889. It is named after engineer Gustave Eiffel. It is made of iron and weighs about 10,000 tonnes! The French affectionately call it the *La dame de fer*, or, the Iron lady.

The **CENTRE POMPIDOU** is a museum, cultural centre and an architecural icon. It was created by architects Richard Rogers, Renzo Piano and Gianfranco Franchini in 1971. It is an 'inside-out' building, with all the pipes, vents and escalators on the outside!

The **MUSÉE D'ORSAY** was originally a grand railway station, built in 1900. Today it is home to both sculptures and *Impressionist* art, and one of Paris' most popular museums.

FAMOUS PARISIANS

WRITERS & POETS
Alexandre Dumas (1802-1870)
Victor Hugo (1802-1885)
Charles Baudelaire (1821-1867)
Guy de Maupassant (1850-1893)
Antoine de Saint-Exupéry (1900-1944)

ARTISTS & MUSICIANS
Édouard Manet (1832-1883)
Edgar Degas (1834-1917)
Claude Monet (1840-1906)
Henri de Toulouse-Lautrec (1864-1901)
Claude Debussy (1862-1918)
Édith Piaf (1915-1963)

SCIENTISTS & INVENTORS
Blaise Pascal (1623-1662)
Antoine Lavoisier (1743-1794)
Jean-Baptiste Lamarck (1744-1829)
Louis Pasteur (1822-1895)

Prague

Prague was an important city for Christianity in the Middle Ages, and later, a place of scientific and cultural innovation. In medieval times it was the capital of Bohemia, a region that is now part of the Czech Republic. Then it became the capital of the Holy Roman Empire, and in the 1500s, capital of the Habsburg Empire. Today, Prague is the capital of the Czech Republic, and its biggest city.

QUICK FACTS

- **Local Name:** Praha
- **Languages:** Mainly Czech, and English
- **CLAIM TO FAME:** Spiritual home of Christianity

Medieval emperor Rudolf II was obsessed with alchemy and science. Under his rule Prague became known as the **GOLDEN CITY.**

Prague is called the **CITY OF A HUNDRED SPIRES,** although it may have closer to 500!

THE GOLDEN AGES OF PRAGUE

During the 14th Century, King Charles IV, laid the foundations of Prague's **New Town** and the University, which was the first in Central Europe. The building of the St Vitus Cathedral and the Charles Bridge began. Other areas around the castle expanded and prospered. Charles was also elected the Holy Roman Emperor in 1355, making Prague the **capital of the Holy Roman Empire.**

Under the Habsburg dynasty in the 1500s, the city saw another period of change. The capital of the empire had been moved to Vienna, but Rudolf II, who was also Holy Roman Emperor, moved it back to Prague. This time, the city attracted many great scientists, musicians and artists, ensuring Prague's status as a cultural capital of Europe.

The **CHARLES BRIDGE** spans the Vltava river, and was built by King Charles IV in the 15th century. It connects the Old Town to the castle, and historically it was very important for trade. 30 statues of saints line the bridge, which is popular with locals and tourists for a leisurely stroll.

Prague Timeline

870	1231	1257	1618-1648
Prague Castle founded	The Old Town (Staré mêsto) is founded	The Lesser Town (Malá Strana) is founded	The Thirty Years' War is fought in Europe and Prague goes into decline

'THE GOOD KING WENCESLAS'

This legendary king of the popular Christmas carol was not a king at all, but the Duke of Bohemia. He was born in Prague in 907 AD, and ruled from 921 till 935, when he was murdered by his own brother Boleslav. The Czech people consider him a very pious figure and a martyr, and he is worshipped as 'Svatý Václave' (Saint Wenceslas).

ST VITUS CATHEDRAL is the seat of the Archbishop of Prague. The building that stands today is the third version of the cathedral! The first was built by Duke Wenceslas in 1344, in the Gothic style. A second, bigger version followed in 1060.

Located in the Old Town, the **Orloj** is an astronomical clock dating back to 1410. It is the oldest working clock in the world.

FAMOUS PRAGUERS

Scientists **TYCHO BRAHE AND JOHANNES KEPLER** worked on major astronomical discoveries in Prague's observatory.

MOZART, though not born in Prague, had strong musical connections to the city in the 18th Century.

ANTONÍN DVORÁK, composer and head of Prague Conservatory was born here in 1841 and died in 1904.

FRANZ KAFKA, the famous writer, was a German-Jewish Praguer, born in 1883 and died in 1924.

PRAGUE CASTLE is the city's most iconic and important building. It dates back to the 9th century, and is the largest ancient castle in the world.

The huge castle complex contains palaces, gardens, churches and towers, all built over centuries in different styles. Today it is home to the President of the Czech Republic, and it is also a UNESCO World Heritage site.

1939-1945

Occupation of Czechoslovakia by Nazi Germany

1945

Prague Offensive, the Soviet army helps end Nazi occupation

1989

Velvet revolution, end of Communism in Czechoslovakia

1993

The Czech Republic is founded

Rome

Rome is famous for being an ancient city, and the fountain of Christianity. It is the capital of Italy, and also of the Province of Rome. Its history spans more than two and a half thousand years, since its legendary founding in 753 BC. Rome is regarded as one of the birthplaces of western civilization.

QUICK FACTS

- **Local Name:** Roma
- **Languages:** Italian
- **CLAIM TO FAME:** Birthplace of Western Civilisation, and home to the Catholic Church

Nearly **€ 70,000** worth of coins are tossed into Rome's Trevi fountain every year by people making a wish!

A COUNTRY IN A CITY

Vatican City is an independent country within Rome, and at hardly 2km across it is also the world's smallest! But to Catholics around the world it is the holiest of places, home to the Pope, and the spiritual heart of Christianity. It is also known for being a tourist magnet, because St Peter's Basilica, possibly the most famous church in the world, stands here. The original basilica was founded by none other than Constantine in the 4th century. The current basilica was worked on by the famous **Michelangelo,** who also painted the ceiling in the Sistine Chapel in 1512. It is built on Vatican Hill, across the Tiber river. It is here that Saint Peter, the chief apostle and first Pope, died a martyr.

According to legend, Rome was founded by **Romulus.** He and his twin Remus were raised by a she-wolf!

Rome is also called the **Eternal City.**

Rome Timeline

753 BC
Rome is allegedly founded by Romulus

390 BC
Rome sacked by Gauls

44 BC
Caesar elects himself dictator, and is killed by Brutus and Cassius

67 AD
St Peter, the first pope, is crucified

1348
Black Death strikes Rome

FIGHT CLUB

The Colosseum is probably the most impressive building in the city. Also known as the *Flavian Amphitheatre*, it was the largest stadium of its time. It could hold 70,000 people, who would come to watch bloody battles between gladiators and wild animals! **Roman gladiators** were mostly convicted criminals, prisoners of war, or slaves. To the audience, dying in 'mortal combat' was no big deal - it was entertainment!

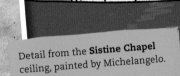

Detail from the **Sistine Chapel** ceiling, painted by Michelangelo.

MICHELANGELO

Michelangelo Buonarroti was born in 1475. He was a painter, sculptor, architect and poet, and is considered the most famous artist of the Italian Renaissance. He lived most of his life in Rome, where he died in 1564 at the age of 88. Michelangelo's crowning glory was being made chief architect of St. Peter's Basilica in 1546.

FAMOUS CEASARS

AUGUSTUS was the first emperor of Rome. His real name was Octavian, but he was called 'Augustus' by the senate as an honour for his great achievements.

JULIUS CAESAR was the most famous Roman of them all. He was also a brilliant general.

CONSTANTINE THE GREAT was the first Christian emperor, who defeated his rivals to reunite the Roman empire.

NERO, called the **THE MADMAN OF ROME**, was the most notorious Caesar of all times. He is supposed to have sung as he watched Rome burn down in the Great fire!

1797
Napoleon captures the city

1870
Rome captured by Kingdom of Italy.

1944
Rome is liberated by Allied troops during World War II

Cappuccino coffee takes its name from the Capuchin monks in Rome, who wear a brown habit!

Stockholm

Stockholm is the capital of Sweden. It is also Sweden's largest city and the source of its commerce and culture. Known for its natural beauty, the city sits upon 13 islands of the lake Mälaren, near the Baltic Sea.

QUICK FACTS

- **Local Name:** Stockholm
- **Languages:** Swedish, Finnish and English
- **CLAIM TO FAME:** Land of the Vikings!

TRADING TOWN

A Swedish king named Birger Jarl is said to have founded Stockholm around 1250 AD. The city was an important centre for international trade, because of its waterways. So for many years, Denmark and Sweden fought to take control of it. In 1523, Swedish nobleman Gustav Vasa finally captured Stockholm, and was crowned King of Sweden. Stockholm became the official capital of Sweden in 1634. The city grew rapidly, and by the middle of the 1700s, Stockholm was the cultural centre of the country.

THE VIKINGS

The Vikings were sea-farers who lived between 700 – 1100 AD. They spoke the Old Norse language, and used their sailing skills to either trade with other countries, or invade them! The name Sweden comes from one of the viking tribes called *Svears*. The Svears led trading expeditions to Russia and Byzantium, and were famous for their **Longboats**.

The name Stockholm means **'log island'** in Swedish.

Stockholm is part of the largest **ARCHIPELAGO** in Sweden, which contains nearly 30,000 islands of all sizes.

Stockholm Timeline

750–790
Trade centre of Birka established on Lake Mälaren

1252
First historic mention of Stockholm

SMÖRGÅSBORD

A Smörgåsbord is the Swedish version of a buffet meal. It contains various hot and cold starters, salads, meats and cheeses. The word itself comes Swedish *Smörgs* (sandwich or bread) and *bord* (board). Now the word just means a 'collection' of anything... like a smörgåsbord of ideas!

Viking helmets did **NOT** have horns!

FAMOUS STOCKHOLMERS

GRETA GARBO (1905-1990)
Actress

INGRID BERGMAN (1915-1982)
Actress

INGMAR BERGMAN (1918-2007)
Film Director and Producer, worked in Stockholm

ASTRID LINDGREN (1907-2002)
Children's Author, creator of *Pippi Longstocking*

THE NOBEL PRIZE

The very prestigious Nobel prize is awarded every year, in the fields of physics, chemistry, medicine, literature, economics, and peace. It honours people who have done outstanding work in one of these areas.

The Nobel Prize is named after Swedish scientist **Alfred Noble,** who invented dynamite!

Gamla Stan is Stockholm's old town, dating back to the 1300s. The King's Palace, Stockholm Cathedral, and the Nobel Museum are all located in this part of the city.

SCANDINAVIAN DESIGN

Scandinavian Design emerged in the 1950s in Sweden, Denmark, Norway, and Finland. It is a design movement based on simplicity and function. The most famous icon of Scandinavian style these days is IKEA, which is a big Swedish furniture company.

Europe

37

1350
Black Death plagues the city

1520
Stockholm bloodbath is ordered by Christian II of Denmark

1719
The city escapes Russian invasion

1986
Prime minister **Olof Palme** is assassinated

It is said that prisoners walking across this bridge for execution would let out a sad sigh... and so the name **'BRIDGE OF SIGHS!'**

It is very difficult to get a licence for operating a **Gondola**... the training and exams are very tough!

Venice Timeline

569
The *Veneti* from northern Italy found Venice

697
Election of first Doge

1082
Venice gets trading privileges from Constantinople, which help her prosper

c. 1495
Venetian printers Nicolas Jenson and Aldus Manutius create 'Roman' and 'Italic' typefaces

c. 1720
Canaletto paints his famous views of the Venetian canals

1866
Venice joins the Italian Kingdom

1934
Mussolini invites Adolf Hitler to Venice

1945
World War II; British Army enters Venice

Venice

Venice is the capital of the Veneto region in Italy. Historically it was the capital of the Republic of Venice, which was a major maritime empire during the Middle Ages. Venice is not a huge city, but it is unique in its architecture and history.

THE FLOATING CITY

The city of Venice is built on water. Instead of roads, there are canals, and people either walk or use boats to get where they want. To make sure that the city was stable, the clever builders of medieval Venice used water-resistant wooden piles, or logs. These were driven below the water and silt, where the ground is mostly clay. Pieces of impermeable rock, like marble, were thrown between the logs, and layers of wood were added on top. Buildings were then constructed above this layer. This method has worked well for centuries, but recently the city has been steadily sinking. This is because of rising sea levels and erosion over time. New technologies are needed to prevent further damage.

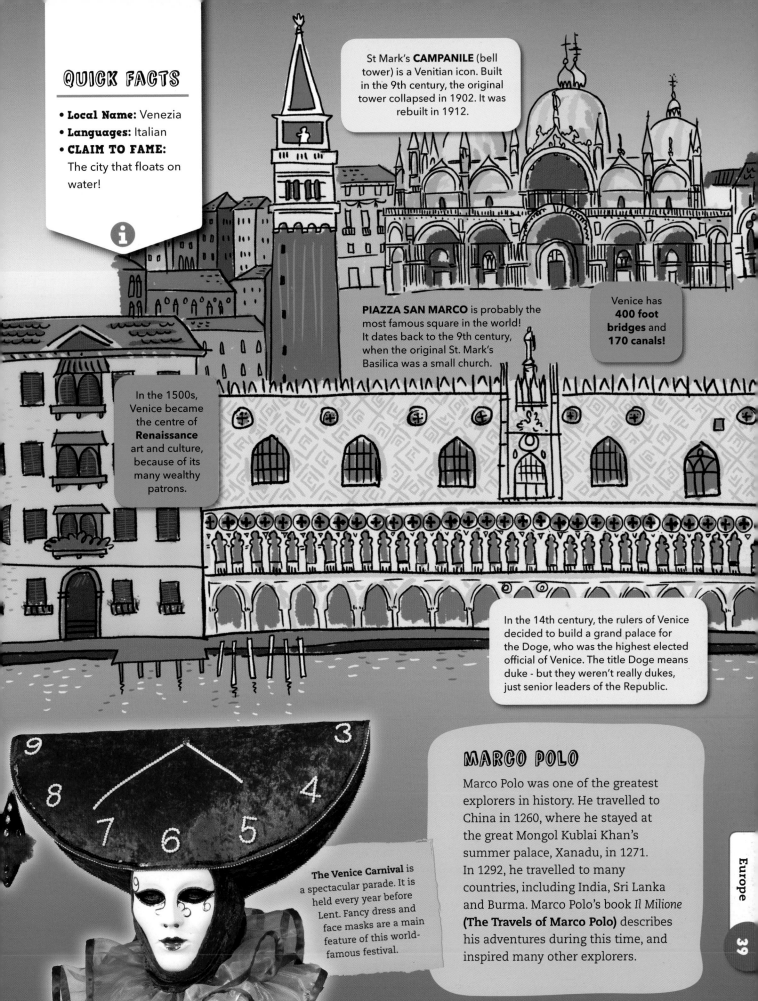

QUICK FACTS

- **Local Name:** Venezia
- **Languages:** Italian
- **CLAIM TO FAME:** The city that floats on water!

St Mark's **CAMPANILE** (bell tower) is a Venitian icon. Built in the 9th century, the original tower collapsed in 1902. It was rebuilt in 1912.

PIAZZA SAN MARCO is probably the most famous square in the world! It dates back to the 9th century, when the original St. Mark's Basilica was a small church.

Venice has **400 foot bridges** and **170 canals!**

In the 1500s, Venice became the centre of **Renaissance** art and culture, because of its many wealthy patrons.

In the 14th century, the rulers of Venice decided to build a grand palace for the Doge, who was the highest elected official of Venice. The title Doge means duke - but they weren't really dukes, just senior leaders of the Republic.

MARCO POLO

Marco Polo was one of the greatest explorers in history. He travelled to China in 1260, where he stayed at the great Mongol Kublai Khan's summer palace, Xanadu, in 1271. In 1292, he travelled to many countries, including India, Sri Lanka and Burma. Marco Polo's book *Il Milione* **(The Travels of Marco Polo)** describes his adventures during this time, and inspired many other explorers.

The Venice Carnival is a spectacular parade. It is held every year before Lent. Fancy dress and face masks are a main feature of this world-famous festival.

Vienna

Vienna is the largest city of Austria, and its capital. It lies on the banks of River Danube, and dates back at least 4000 years. It is famous for its history, and its elegant architecture. Many of the city's buildings are ornate, and create a feeling of majesty. Vienna has always been an important power in Europe.

STEPHANSDOM
(St Stephen's Cathedral) was built in 1147 and is an icon of Vienna.

Vienna still holds around 200 **Ball dances** every year, in its many beautiful palaces.

The Kiss, by Secessionist artist Gustav Klimt in 1907. These gilded paintings were from his 'Golden Period'.

ART AND MUSIC IN VIENNA

Vienna is called the World Capital of Music. It is best known for classical music. Some of its most prolific composers include Wolfgang Amadeus Mozart, Joseph Haydn, Ludwig van Beethoven, Johann Strauss and Franz Schubert. Vienna is home to many musical theatres and opera houses.

The Secession: In 1897, some painters, sculptors, and architects came together to form a movement called the 'Vienna Secession'. Among them were names like Gustav Klimt and Josef Hoffman.

Vienna sits along the **Danube**, Europe's second-longest river after the Volga.

THE HAPSBURGS

The Hapsburgs were originally originally a noble family from Switzerland, but went on to become the greatest ruling dynasty in Europe for over 500 years. They used marriage and politics, rather than war, to gain new territories. The Hapsburgs were also elected Holy Roman Emperors. The dynasty's influence was spread over Germany, Spain, Italy, Hungary, and of course, Austria. Emperor Friedrich III is famous for the inscription AEIOU ("*Alles Erdreich Ist Österreich Untertan*", meaning: the whole world is subject to Austria) which adorned many buildings of his time. Maria Theresa, their only female ruler, was the last of the House of Hapsburg. She was also Holy Roman Empress! She ruled for 40 successful years, till 1780.

Schloss Belvedere is a Baroque palace with grand, formal gardens. It now houses the Belvedere Museum.

FAMOUS VIENNESE

JOHANN STRAUSS II (1825-1899) Prolific composer, creator of *Blue Danube Waltz*

WOLFGANG AMADEUS MOZART (1756-1791) The most famous composer of all time, worked in Vienna.

SIGMUND FREUD (1856-1939) Psychiatrist and neurologist, known as the 'father of psychoanalysis'.

Vienna Timeline

500 BC
Celtic fortress Vedunia is founded in present-day Vienna

15 BC
Vedunia is ruled by Romans, and renamed Vindobona

995 AD
Vienna prospers under Otto the Great, of the Babenberg dynasty

1278
The Habsburg dynasty takes over. Vienna becomes capital of the Austro-Hungarian empire

1529-1683
Ottomans repeatedly try to beseige Vienna, but it survives

1848
Vienna is modernised after the Revolution of 1848

1914
Archduke Franz Ferdinand is assassinated. World War I follows

1955
Austria becomes an independent country

Zurich resident **Johanna Spryi** wrote **HEIDI**, the popular children's story about a little girl who lives in the Alps with her grandfather.

Zurich, is the **largest city** on Zurichsee (Lake Zurich).

Zurich

Zurich is an ancient town, and there is evidence of Stone Age and Bronze Age settlements around Lake Zurich. Later on the Romans settled in an area near the Limmat River, and called the town Turicum. In modern times, Zurich has become a financial powerhouse, and today it is Switzerland's biggest city.

People gather around Zurich's famous **'singing tree.'** Christmas here is a magical time, with bright lights, and Europe's best christmas markets.

The Latin name of Switzerland is **CONFOEDERATIO HELVETICA**. That's why Swiss websites end in .CH.

NATURAL BEAUTY

Zurich sits on the northern tip of Lake Zurich, or Zurichsee. It is also on very near to the Alps. The snowy Alps cover more than 60% of Switzerland, making it a very mountainous country! Like many Swiss towns and cities, Zurich is surrounded by scenic beauty.

Zurich is famous for its **fine chocolates!**

Zurich Timeline

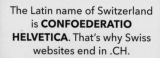

c.100 AD	1351	1522	1855	1799	1945
Turicum founded by Romans	Zurich joins Swiss confederation.	'The Affair of the Sausages' leads to Reformation in Switzerland.	Stock exchange established.	First and Second Battles of Zurich (France versus Russia and Austria)	Bombing by United States.

42

QUICK FACTS

- **Local Name:** Zurich
- **Languages:** German and French
- **CLAIM TO FAME:** Rich banks, and richer chocolates!

James Joyce wrote **ULYSSES** in Zurich.

The clock of St. Peter's Church is the **largest church clock face** in Europe.

Zurich's iconic Grossmünster is where Huldrych Zwingli, father of Swiss Protestantism, began preaching the **REFORMATION** in 1519.

Fraumünster Church has some stained glass windows designed by renowned artist **Marc Chagall.**

MONEY MONEY MONEY!

Zurich is famous for being a tax haven, and is the wealthiest city in Europe. Historically, many Swiss men fought as mercenaries for the French army. They brought home wealth which helped in the founding of the first Swiss Banks. Over the years, because of lower taxes and relaxed rules, the world's super-rich opened 'offshore' accounts here. Today, almost 30% of all offshore wealth is kept in Swiss banks!

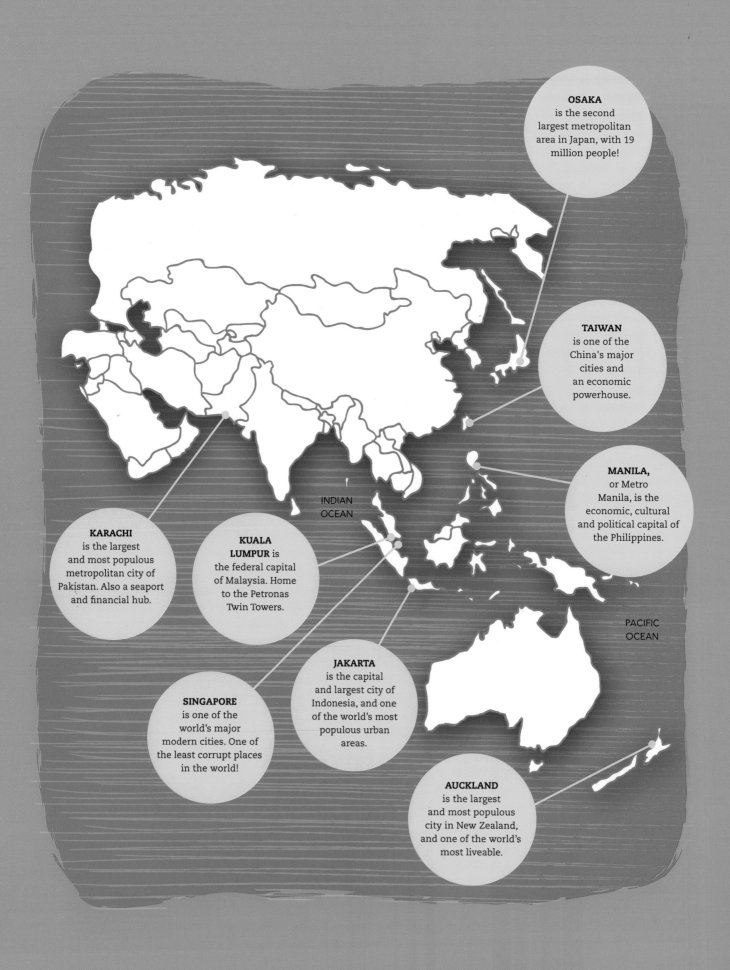

OSAKA is the second largest metropolitan area in Japan, with 19 million people!

TAIWAN is one of the China's major cities and an economic powerhouse.

MANILA, or Metro Manila, is the economic, cultural and political capital of the Philippines.

KARACHI is the largest and most populous metropolitan city of Pakistan. Also a seaport and financial hub.

KUALA LUMPUR is the federal capital of Malaysia. Home to the Petronas Twin Towers.

INDIAN OCEAN

PACIFIC OCEAN

SINGAPORE is one of the world's major modern cities. One of the least corrupt places in the world!

JAKARTA is the capital and largest city of Indonesia, and one of the world's most populous urban areas.

AUCKLAND is the largest and most populous city in New Zealand, and one of the world's most liveable.

Great Cities of

ASIA AND AUSTRALIA

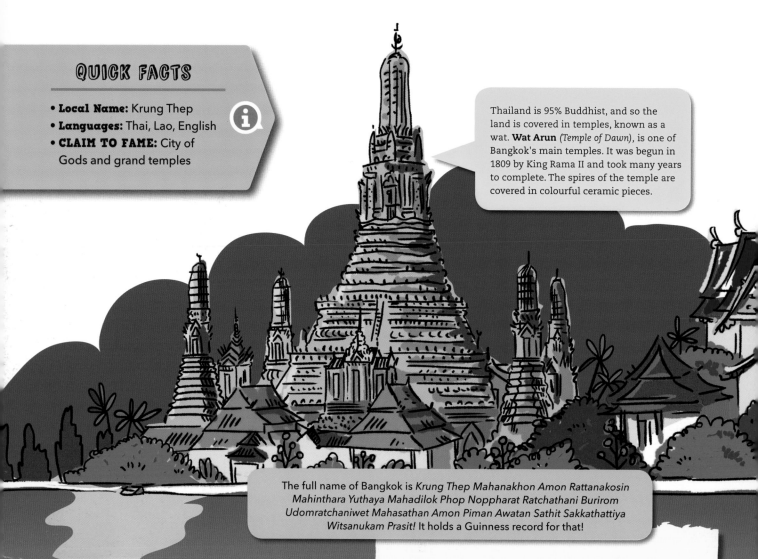

QUICK FACTS

- **Local Name:** Krung Thep
- **Languages:** Thai, Lao, English
- **CLAIM TO FAME:** City of Gods and grand temples

Thailand is 95% Buddhist, and so the land is covered in temples, known as a wat. **Wat Arun** *(Temple of Dawn)*, is one of Bangkok's main temples. It was begun in 1809 by King Rama II and took many years to complete. The spires of the temple are covered in colourful ceramic pieces.

The full name of Bangkok is *Krung Thep Mahanakhon Amon Rattanakosin Mahinthara Yuthaya Mahadilok Phop Noppharat Ratchathani Burirom Udomratchaniwet Mahasathan Amon Piman Awatan Sathit Sakkathattiya Witsanukam Prasit!* It holds a Guinness record for that!

Bangkok

Bangkok is the capital of Thailand, and its largest city. It began as a small trading town on the banks of the Chao Phraya River 200 years ago. A modern city surrounded by its vivid history, Bangkok is now the country's main port.

CITY OF PLUMS, AND GODS...

Bangkok became capital of Siam in 1782. General Chakri, of the Chakri dynasty, assumed the throne as King Rama I and moved his court to the west bank of the Chao Praya river. He modelled the new city on the old capital of Ayutthaya. The name Bangkok probably comes from **bang** (village) and **makok** (of wild plums). The Thai call the city *Krung Thep,* meaning **City of Gods.**

In the 19th century, the French and British presence in Siam increased. The modernisation of the city was based on Thai admiration for the West. Later, Bangkok came under Japanese occupation, and Allied bombing during World War II. But after the war, the city developed into a metropolis.

Bangkok Timeline

c 14th century
Settlement of Bangkok

1688
Siamese revolution/ Siege of Bangkok, French traders are expelled from country

1782
Bangkok becomes the capital of Siam

Bangkok's **Grand Palace** is the official residence of the Kings of Siam (old name of Thailand). It was built by King Rama I of the Chakri dynasty in 1782, when the capital moved from Thonburi to Bangkok. The palace complex contains many buildings.

Every April Bangkok hosts the world's largest street water fight during the **Songkran Festival,** Thailand's New Year.

VENICE OF THE EAST

Bangkok has always relied on its waterways for transport and trade. It has been compared to Venice because of its many canals, called *khlong* in Thai. In the 20th century, many of these khlongs were filled in and made into roads, as part of the city's modernisation. But the remaining khlongs are still used to bring in goods to the city's popular **floating markets.**

1820	1932	1941–45	1998
Cholera pandemic kills 30,000	Coup ends absolute monarchy	Bombing of Bangkok in World War II	Bangkok hosts Asian Games

Beijing

Beijing is a truly ancient city, dating back to more than 400,000 years! For the last 800 years, it has been the capital of China. This city has a tumultuous, imperial history, but it is also crucial to the modern world with its booming economy.

QUICK FACTS

- **Local Name:** Beijing
- **Languages:** Mandarin (Beijing dialect)
- **CLAIM TO FAME:** Imperial grandeur, and a powerful modern economy.

The Forbidden City, Summer Palace, and the Temple of Heaven are **UNESCO World Heritage Sites**.

ANCIENT CITADEL OF CHINA

Beijing has been a special city for millennia. The earliest settlement here was in 1050 BC. Around 450 BC, it was the capital of the **Yan** dynasty, and called Ji. In the 1200s, the great Mongol ruler **Kublai Khan** built a city here, called Dadu, and made it China's capital.

In the 1360s, the city came under **Ming** rule. The Forbidden City (the Imperial Palace) was begun under the Mings, and the rest of city was built according to feng-shui principles. In 1421 it got its current name, Beijing, meaning 'northern capital.'

The **Qing** dynasty took over in 1644, and Beijing prospered. In the 1800s, however, foreign powers encroached on the city. The palaces were burnt down in the Opium wars between the British and the French. The Boxer Rebellion caused more destruction in the 1890s.

After being ruled by the **Kuomintang** (Nationalist Party) and the Japanese for some time, Beijing finally came under the communist rule of **Mao Zedong.** It became the capital of the People's Republic of China in 1949.

Beijing Timeline

c.1000 BC
Kingdoms of *Yah* and *Ji* are established in Beijing area

618 AD
Garrison town of Youzhou under *Tang Dynasty*

1271
Dadu, Capital of the Yuan Dynasty

Peking Man (*Homo erectus pekinensis*), is an example of a prehistoric human. His remains were discovered in 1923-27 during excavations at Zhoukoudian near Beijing. Peking Man stood erect, made stone tools, and used fire.

Beijing was called **PEKING** in the West till the 1980s.

People in Beijing speak **Beijinghua**, a unique dialect of Mandarin.

MAO ZEDONG

Mao Zedong was the founding father of the People's Republic of China, and its chairman from 1949 to 1959. He led the Chinese Communist Party from 1935 until his death. His two strategies - the 'Great Leap Forward' and the 'Cultural Revolution' - were very controversial, but he believed that China should become a self-reliant and confident country.

MODERN BEIJING

Beijing was modernised by the communist government, and the city expanded. Its imperial image gave way to contemporary buildings and a flourishing electronics industry. The city's architecture and economy was boosted by the 2008 Olympics, when 31 venues were built just for the games. Modern Beijing is still the seat of politics and culture in China, but it is also a hub of international activity.

FAMOUS BEIJINGERS

XI JINPING (b-1953)
President of the People's Republic of China

JET LI (b-1963)
Actor, producer and martial artist

AI WEIWEI (b-1957)
World renowned contemporary artist

ZHANG ZIYI (b-1979)
Actress and model

The Great Wall was built over centuries, and the parts close to Beijing are the best preserved.

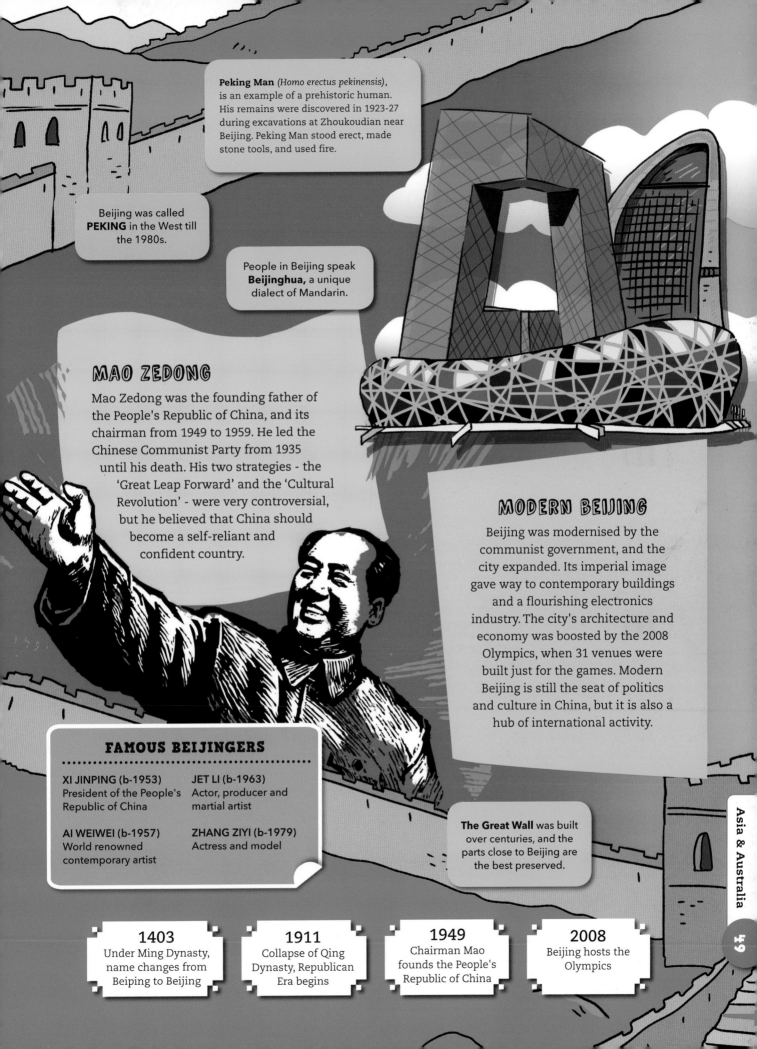

49

1403	1911	1949	2008
Under Ming Dynasty, name changes from Beiping to Beijing	Collapse of Qing Dynasty, Republican Era begins	Chairman Mao founds the People's Republic of China	Beijing hosts the Olympics

Delhi

Delhi, or New Delhi, is the capital of India. It is one the oldest urban settlements in the world, with evidence of people living there as early as the 6th century BC. Because of its unique position in northern India, it has always played an important political part. An old saying is that "He who rules Delhi, rules India."

QUICK FACTS

- **Local Name:** Dilli
- **Languages:** Hindi, Punjabi, Urdu and English
- **CLAIM TO FAME:** Prized location and a layered history.

Legend has it that Delhi was once the famous city of **INDRAPRASTHA**, named in the Sanskrit epic *Mahabharata*.

Delhi is one of the world's **most populous** cities.

Delhiites own a total of almost **7 million cars!**

FAMOUS DELHIITES

MIRZA GHALIB (1797-1869) Delhi's most renowned poet, who wrote in Urdu and Persian

AMIR KHUSRO (1253-1325), Sufi poet and mystic

KHUSHWANT SINGH (1915-2014) Prominent novelist, journalist and politician.

SHAHRUKH KHAN, popular *Bollywood* actor, was born here in 1965.

Standing 73 meters high, the Qutb Minar is the **tallest brick minaret in the world.** It was built by Qutbuddin Aibak, the first Sultan of Delhi, in 1192.

'CITIES' OF DELHI

Delhi's long history is best explained by its eight 'cities.' Almost every ruler who controlled large parts of India, chose Delhi as its capital. As a result, the city is full of old monuments from different eras, some still in good shape, some almost gone.

QILA RAI PITHORA
The **RAJPUT CHAUHANS** ruled the area in the 10th century, and this was the 'first' city of Delhi.

MEHRAULI
Then came the **SLAVE DYNASTY** of Mohammad of Ghor. This was the first Muslim dynasty in Delhi, ruling till 1296. They built mosques, and victory towers.

SIRI
The **KHILJI DYNASTY** ruled from 1296 till 1315 and built the Siri fort, and a massive water tank called Hauz Khas.

TUGHLAQABAD
Ghiyas-ud-din, of the **TUGHLAQ DYNASTY**, built a huge fort, which contained the 'fourth city.'

JAHANPANAH
This fort was built by Muhammad-bin-Tughlaq, but nothing much remains of this building now.

GREEN CITY

Almost 20% of Delhi is covered in trees, making it one of the greenest cities in the world. The forested Ridge area in the city supports a unique flora and fauna. It is almost 1,500 million years old, and is called the 'lungs of Delhi.'

Delhi has the second highest number of birds, out of all world capitals!

Autorickshaws are a popular mode of transport in Delhi. The city runs its public transport on eco-friendly Natural Gas fuel.

Delhi sits on the banks of the **Yamuna**, one of India's holy rivers.

Mughal emperor **HUMAYUN'S TOMB** was built in 1569. The design for the famous *Taj Mahal* is said to be inspired by it.

The stone pillar at Firozshah Kotla belongs to **ASHOKA THE GREAT**, and dates back to the 3rd century BC.

URDU, a language spoken by a 100 million people in South Asia, evolved in Delhi.

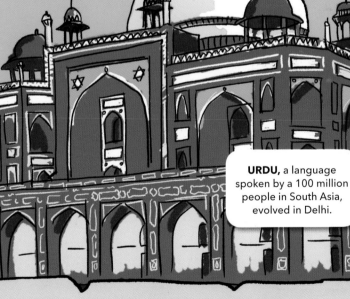

Delhi Timeline

736 AD
Anangpal Tomar founds 'Dhilli.'

1911
King George V declared Delhi the new capital of India, replacing Calcutta.

Aug 15, 1947
India becomes independent. The partition of India and Pakistan brings almost a million migrants into Delhi.

1948
Mahatma Gandhi is assassinated in the city.

1982
New Delhi hosts the Asian Games

1984
Prime Minister Indira Gandhi is assassinated, leading to riots in the city.

1991
New Delhi is granted statehood and renamed the National Capital Territory of Delhi

2001
A terrorist attack on the Indian Parliament kills 14 people

2010
New Delhi hosts the Commonwealth Games

FIROZSHAH KOTLA
Firozeshah Tughlaq built a fort on the banks of the river Yamuna, and this is considered the fifth city of Delhi.

SHERGARH/DINPANAH
Mughal ruler Humayun built a fort called *Dinpanah*. It was captured by Sher Shah Suri, a warrior from central India, but soon Humayun won it back.

SHAHJEHANABAD
The Mughal emperor Shah Jehan built the famous Red Fort in 1648. The area around it is called Old Delhi, which is considered the seventh city of Delhi.

NEW DELHI
The British built up central 'new' Delhi in the style of European capitals, with the Parliament House and the Presidential P alace, and many other official structures. This area is considered the eighth city of Delhi.

Dubai

Dubai is part of the United Arab Emirates (UAE), a group of seven Arab kingdoms in the Arabian Peninsula. It is a major financial centre, and it is very wealthy because of the oil reserves in the area. Nowadays the city is renowned for being a luxury destination.

BURJ KHALIFA is over 828 metres (2,716.5 feet) tall and has 164 floors.

The shape of the luxury hotel **BURJ AL ARAB** is inspired by the sail of a ship.

TALLEST, BIGGEST, RICHEST!

Dubai can boast many records. It is the largest city in the UAE. Its metro system, is the largest automated rail network in the world, with 87 driver-less trains! It has the world's largest shopping mall. It also has the world's most luxurious hotel, the 7-star **Burj Al-Arab.** The **Dubai World Cup,** an annual horse race, is the world's richest horse race. with a prize of USD 10 million! The **Palm Jumeirah** is the world's largest artificial island, and can be seen from space. And it now has the world's tallest building, the **Burj Khalifa!** The list goes on...

The **ATLANTIS** resort and hotel stands on the island of Palm Jumeirah.

Dubai has no postal codes! Everyone's mail is delivered to local post boxes, where they go and collect it.

Dubai has a strong identity, but not even 15% of the people who live here are actually Emiratis (UAE citizens)! Immigrants make up most of the population, and the majority of these are labourers, coming in to work on the various building projects around the growing city. Half of the people living in Dubai are Indians or of Indian descent!

- **Local Name:** Dubai, Dubayy
- **Languages:** Arabic and English
- **CLAIM TO FAME:** Luxury destination for the rich and famous!

Dubai is one of the safest places on earth, with strict laws and a near 0% crime rate!

THE HISTORY

Historically, the Dubai area was settled circa 3000 BC, by nomadic herders. From around 300 AD it was ruled by the **Sassanid Empire,** which hailed from Persia (Iran), and later by the **Umayyads,** who introduced Islam to the region. Dubai proper, was established in the 19th century by the **Al-Falasi** dynasty. It became a separate 'sheikhdom' in 1833.

Dubai had a good fishing trade, and also exported pearls to the world. In the 1960s, oil reserves were discovered, which greatly increased its fortunes. In fact, because of its oil exports, Dubai was soon very important within the Emirates, and became an independent state.

Today, Dubai's Emir (ruler) is **Sheikh Mohammed.** Under his rule the city gained global prominence, and became not just a commercial, but a cultural destination too.

Dubai is surrounded by the **ARABIAN DESERT.**

Dubai has many man-made islands. There's one in the shape of a large palm tree, called **Palm Jumeirah,** and it is home to resorts, hotels, restaurants and private homes. The Al-Burj hotel stands on an artificial island too.

Dubai Timeline

500 AD
Sassanids set up trading post in Jumeira

632
Islam spreads in the region, people speak Arabic

1590
Gasparo Balbi, of Venice, writes about a fishing village called 'Dibei'

1853
The *Perpetual Treaty of Maritime Truce* is signed by Britain and local sheikhs

1969
Oil production begins

1971
The UAE becomes an independent federation

2008
Recession hits Dubai, stalling many projects.

Hong Kong

Hong Kong sits on the south-east coast of China, jutting out into the South China Sea. Its deep harbour makes it a valuable shipping port. Hong Kong is known as the world's first global city, with soaring skyscrapers and an international mix of people.

The iconic **Bank of China Tower** was designed by renowned architect I. M. Pei.

Hong Kong owns the world's most skyscrapers, more than 7,000! Land is precious and expensive on this island, and the only way to build is up!

JUNK BOATS are ancient Chinese sailing ships, designed for the sea. They were developed during the Song dynasty in the 10th century, and were used for cargo and for transportation. The name 'junk', probably comes from the Chinese word *chuán,* and today these boats are used to ferry people across the Hong Kong waters.

A SPECIAL CITY

The islands of Hong Kong have been settled since the 7th century, when the great **Han dynasty** ruled China. The first Europeans to arrive here were the Portuguese, in 1513. But they were driven out, and replaced, by the British East India Company in 1669. In 1842, Britain took control of Hong Kong, and established a port here. Trade with Europe grew.

When mainland China became communist, many people fled to Hong Kong. In 1997, after 150 years, China gained Hong Kong back from the British. It became a Special Administrative Region of China (**SAR**), and kept its own laws, politics and even currency. Today, Hong Kong continues to be a major financial centre in Asia-Pacific.

THE PEAK

More than anything, Hong Kong is famous for its skyline. And for years, people have been climbing 'the peak' for spectacular views of this 'vertical city'. The proper name for the mountain, which is the highest in Hong Kong, is **Victoria Peak.** It is popular with locals and tourists, and in the 1800s, it was coveted by the British officials as a green spot to build their summer homes.

Hong Kong is the original home of **KUNG FU** movies. **Bruce Lee, Jackie Chan,** and **Jet Li,** all started out with movies produced here. So did the **Teenage Mutant Ninja Turtles**!

The Dragon Boat Race is an ancient Chinese festival, celebrated every year in Hong Kong's Victoria Harbour.

Hong Kong Timeline

1842
China cedes Hong Kong to Britain

1941
Japan occupies Hong Kong

1946
Britain re-establishes its government

1970s
Hong Kong becomes an economic powerhouse

1997
Hong Kong is handed back to China after more than 150 years of British rule

2003
Hong Kong and China are hit by the SARS virus outbreak.

2014
Thousands of protesters take part in pro-democracy rally

QUICK FACTS

- **Local Name:** Hong Kong
- **Languages:** English, Chinese
- **CLAIM TO FAME:** A view to die for!

Melbourne

Melbourne, a multicultural city, is the second biggest in Australia. It is also the capital of the state of Victoria. Melbourne is quite a young city, founded in 1835, when businessmen bought land from the local Aborigines.

FAMOUS MELBOURNIANS

CATE BLANCHETT (b-1969) Actress and Academy Award winner

KYLIE MINOGUE (b-1968) Pop star and actress

PAT CASH (b-1965) Tennis player, Wimbledon champion

SHANE WARNE (b-1969) Cricketer

Melbourne was originally named **Batmania!**

The Melbourne Rectangular Stadium (AAMI Park) features a **geodesic dome** design.

A CONTROVERSIAL BEGINNING

Melbourne was inhabited by groups of Aboriginal people when John Batman arrived here in 1835. By giving them a few small gifts, he thought he had purchased their land. The Aborigines thought they were only letting him pass through. It was later declared an illegal sale! But Batman stayed, and the settlement was named Melbourne. By 1861, the discovery of gold made it the fastest growing city in the British Empire. Many fine buildings and houses came up, including the Flinders Street Station.

QUICK FACTS

- **Local Name:** Melbourne
- **Languages:** English
- **CLAIM TO FAME:** A very sporty city!

The Yarra river was so filthy with sewage in the 1800s that Melbourne was called 'Smellbourne'!

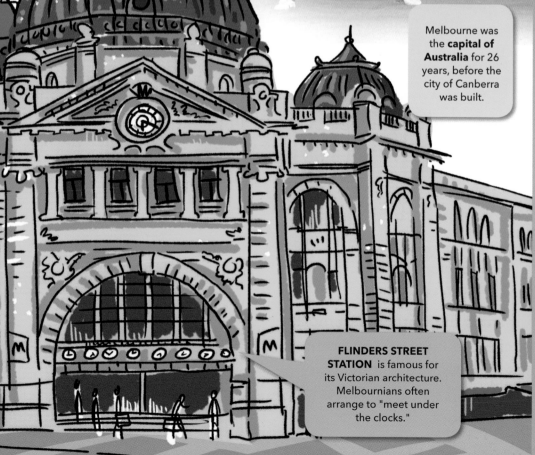

NED KELLY

Ned Kelly was the most notorious bushranger (rural outlaws). His gang committed a spree of armed robberies. Kelly became a folk hero to the Australian public because of his defiance against the police. He was captured in 1878 and imprisoned at Old Melbourne Goal. Kelly was hanged in 1880, but remains a popular figure in Australian history. His last words were: "Such is life".

The very popular **Australian Rules Football** was invented in Melbourne. The Australian Football League (AFL) has 18 teams with a huge fan base.

Melbourne was the **capital of Australia** for 26 years, before the city of Canberra was built.

FLINDERS STREET STATION is famous for its Victorian architecture. Melbournians often arrange to "meet under the clocks."

Melbourne Timeline

1835
The city of Melbourne is founded

1853
Melbourne University is created

1854
A railway is built between Melbourne and Port Melbourne

1878
The first telephone call in Australia is made in Melbourne

1880
Ned Kelly is hanged in Melbourne

1956
Melbourne hosts the Olympic Games

2006
UNESCO designates Melbourne a City of Literature

QUICK FACTS

- **Local Name:** Mumbai
- **Languages:** Marathi, Hindi, English
- **CLAIM TO FAME:** Home to the biggest movie industry in the world!

BOLLYWOOD

Mumbai is home to the world's biggest film industry. The first film made here was in 1913, and today, about 1,000 Hindi language films are produced every year. Almost every Hindi film is about 2 hours long or more, and is a 'masala' mix: a spicy blend of music, dance, romance, action and comedy! Bollywood has its own awards which are very coveted.

Amitabh Bachchan is the most celebrated Bollywood actor. He became famous for his action films in the 1970s and was given the nickname 'angry young man'.

The Portuguese gave Bombay to the English in 1661, as a part of a royal dowry!

People in India are crazy about **CRICKET,** and Mumbai is home to some the best known players, like **Sachin Tendulkar** and **Sunil Gavaskar.**

The seafront monument known as the **GATEWAY OF INDIA** was built in 1911 to welcome King George V to india.

Dharavi in Mumbai used to be an island, today is one of the largest slums in Asia.

Mumbai

The port city of Mumbai is the world's fifth most populous, and the richest in India. It is the capital of the Indian state of Maharashtra, and named after the goddess Mumba. Dynamic and vibrant, it is the country's cultural soul.

Mumbai's old name was Bombay, derived from the Portuguese Bom Bahia, which means **'the Good Bay'.**

Mumbai's **MONSOONS** are legendary. Heavy rain and wind lash the sea and the city, turning streets into rivers!

FAMOUS MUMBAIKARS

LATA MANGESHKAR (b-1929)
Bollywood playback singer

ZUBIN MEHTA (b-1936)
Musical conductor

RATAN TATA (b-1940)
Chairman of Tata Group

ADI GODREJ (b-1942)
Chairman of Godrej Group

MUMBAI'S SUPERHEROES

Mumbai's 'dabbawallas' (lunch delivery men) are renowned for their efficiency. Every day they collect home-cooked hot food in *dabbas* (tiffins) from a customer's home, and deliver it to their office. The empty boxes are returned later that day or the next. The century-old system is almost like a postal service. Even though many *dabbawallas* are not literate, they are very punctual and precise, with a record of less than one error per one million deliveries!

LOCAL RAILWAYS

Local railways are the lifeline of Mumbai. At peak times, you'll find 500 people squashed into carriages meant for just 200! There is even a *Ladies Special* service, where women can travel in safety and also manage to do household chores, like peel vegetables, on the evening train home!

Ganesh Utsav is an annual festival, honouring Lord Ganesha. The elephant-god is worshipped for 10 days, before a procession carries him to be submerged into water. It is Mumbai's most iconic festival, full of colour and splendour.

Mumbai is one of the top 10 cities ranked by their number of **billionnaires**!

Mumbai Timeline

600 BC
First known permanent settlement by the Marathi speaking Koli community

300 BC
Part of Ashoka's Empire

1343
Mumbai is part of the Gujarat sultanate

1670
First printing press imported to Mumbai by Parsi businessman Bhimjee Parikh

1870
Mumbai Port Trust formed

1942
Quit India Movement declaration passed at Gowalia Tank Maidan

1993
Serial bomb blasts across Mumbai kill 300 people

2008
Terrorist attacks across Mumbai kill 164 people

Seoul

Seoul is located on the Korean Peninsula, near the western coast. It is South Korea's largest metropolis. Officially called the *Seoul Special City,* it is the country's political, creative and economic capital.

THE ORIGINAL 'TIGER'

Seoul has been a royal capital since the 14th century. The **Joseon Dynasty** recognised Seoul's good location between a river and the mountains, and built palaces, temples, shrines and fortresses. Unfortunately, when the Japanese Empire annexed Seoul in 1910, many of these buildings were destroyed. Only a few stand today as reminders of the Joseons.

Seoul suffered further in the Korean civil war soon after. In 1945, the country was divided between North and South Korea. Afterwards, with the backing of America, South Korea recovered its economy and became part of the developed world, all within 20 years! It became the original 'Asian Tiger' economy, and can boast of an affluent society today.

Seoul is divided by the **Han River** and surrounded by mountains.

Guards wear colourful uniforms during a pageant at **Gyeongbokgung Palace** in Seoul.

SMART CITY!

Seoul is said to be the most connected and high-tech city in the world. 95% of homes have high speed broadband! Homeowners can control all the devices in the house with their smartphones. Then there's T-money, an electronic currency used to pay for a lot of services including public transport. People also use the UPass, a contact-less smart card. South Korea is home to Electronics giants like Samsung, Hyundai and LG.

Bongeunsa Buddhist temple stands in the busy Gangnam district. This Buddha statue is the tallest in Korea.

The name Seoul probably comes from the Korean word for capital city, **Seorabeol**.

Over half of Korea's population lives in Seoul greater metropolitan area!

Built in the 1300s **Gyeongbokgung Palace** is Korea's most famous royal palace.

Seoul Timeline

1600 BC
Part of Baekje kingdom

1394
Capital of Joseon Dynasty

1395
Gyeongbokgung Palace built

1900s
Railways begin operation from Seoul

1910
Japanese in power; Seoul renamed Keijo

1988
Seoul hosts the Olympics

2002
Seoul hosts the FIFA World Cup

ℹ QUICK FACTS

- **Local Name:** Seoul
- **Languages:** Korean
- **CLAIM TO FAME:** The most tech-savvy city in the world!

Shanghai

Shanghai is one of the world's largest cities by population. Its geographical location was key to its rise as an economic power. It is China's most modern and cosmopolitan city, and one of the greatest in the country.

Shanghai has the world's most extensive bus system, with over **1400** routes!

QUICK FACTS

- **Local Name:** Hu, Shanghai
- **Languages:** Mandarin
- **CLAIM TO FAME:** Busy, busy port!

The main language spoken in Shanghai is **Shanghainese,** which is one of 248 Chinese dialects.

The name Shanghai comes from the Chinese characters *Shang* = above, and *Hai* = sea, meaning **'Upon the Sea'**.

HUANGPU RIVER

Huangpu River is the main river of Shanghai, snaking 70 miles across the city. It is a branch of the famous **Yangtze,** the longest river in China. From Shanghai, it flows into the East China Sea, creating a natural harbour. It is because of this lucky location, that Shanghai can boast the world's busiest sea port! On the east bank of the Huangpu is the **Bund**. Many of its buildings were constructed in the 1920s and 30s, in *Art Deco* and *Neo-Classical* styles. With its grand architecture and bright lights, it is a symbol of Shanghai's modernity and power.

Shanghai Port handles more than **730 million tonnes** of freight every year!

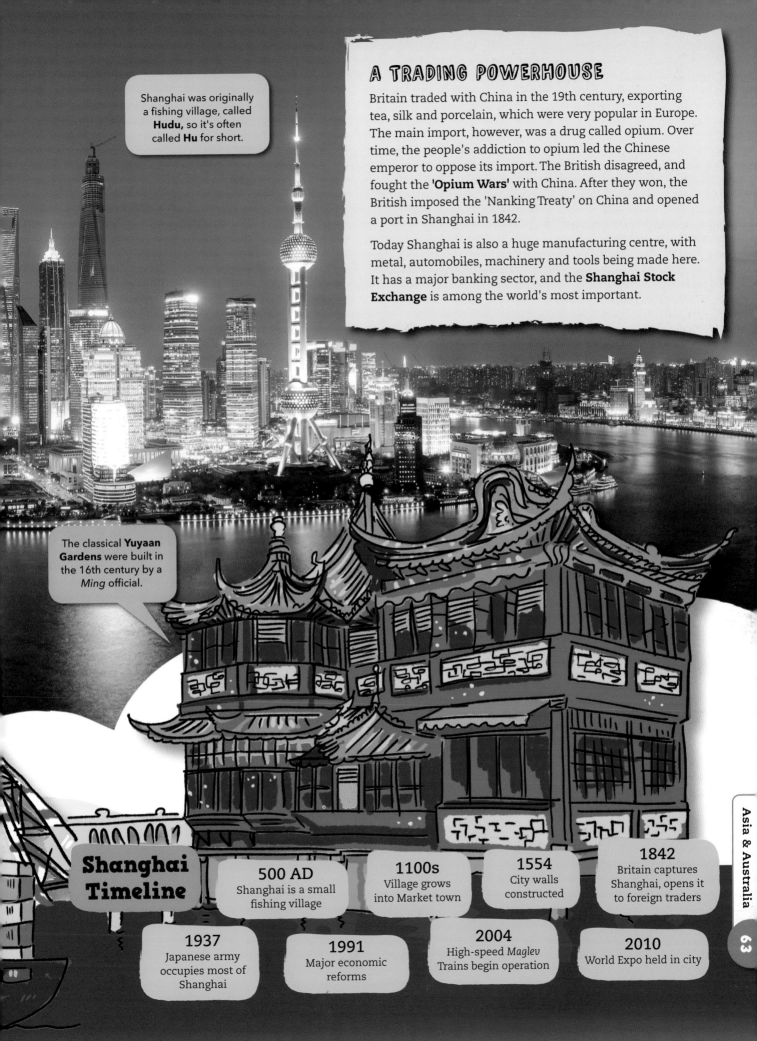

Shanghai was originally a fishing village, called **Hudu,** so it's often called **Hu** for short.

A TRADING POWERHOUSE

Britain traded with China in the 19th century, exporting tea, silk and porcelain, which were very popular in Europe. The main import, however, was a drug called opium. Over time, the people's addiction to opium led the Chinese emperor to oppose its import. The British disagreed, and fought the **'Opium Wars'** with China. After they won, the British imposed the 'Nanking Treaty' on China and opened a port in Shanghai in 1842.

Today Shanghai is also a huge manufacturing centre, with metal, automobiles, machinery and tools being made here. It has a major banking sector, and the **Shanghai Stock Exchange** is among the world's most important.

The classical **Yuyaan Gardens** were built in the 16th century by a *Ming* official.

Shanghai Timeline

500 AD
Shanghai is a small fishing village

1100s
Village grows into Market town

1554
City walls constructed

1842
Britain captures Shanghai, opens it to foreign traders

1937
Japanese army occupies most of Shanghai

1991
Major economic reforms

2004
High-speed *Maglev* Trains begin operation

2010
World Expo held in city

Sydney

Sydney is the largest and oldest city in Australia. It is the capital of the state of New South Wales, and is set on the south-eastern coast. It is Australia's largest metropolitan area, and a very important economic and cultural hub.

During the 18th century, the British government decided to set up penal colonies in newly-discovered Australia. (At that time Australia was called **New Holland**). Over the next 100 years, large numbers of convicts from England were sent there. In 1786, a party of colonists sailed from Portsmouth, which included 775 convicts. They established the first colony in Australia, and that area today is Sydney.

QUICK FACTS

- **Local Name:** Sydney
- **Languages:** English
- **CLAIM TO FAME:** Beaches and the great outdoors!

The arrival of Europeans had an adverse impact on the Aborigines, the original inhabitants of Australia who had been there for 50,000 years! Aborigines had no immunity to the diseases brought by the settlers. Their population in the area declined rapidly. Sydney, however, continued to thrive and expand in the 19th century. Today, Sydney is a huge, multicultural city, with many immigrants from Europe and Asia.

In 1955, Jorn Utzon, an architect from Denmark, won a competition to design the **SYDNEY OPERA HOUSE.** Inspired by boat sails, this iconic building is now a UNESCO World Heritage site.

Sydney is named after British politician **Lord Thomas Townshend**, 1st Viscount Sydney.

THE HARBOUR

Sydney is famous for its huge harbour. It is the **deepest natural harbour** in the world, and is known by the locals as "The Coat Hanger" due to its distinct shape. Its most famous landmarks are the Sydney Harbour Bridge and the Opera House.

Sydney Timeline

1788
The first colonists arrive at Port Jackson

1793
The first free settlers arrive.

1808
The Rum Rebellion takes place

1850
Sydney University is founded

1900
Bubonic plague kills 103 people in Sydney

1973
Sydney Opera House opens

2000
The Olympic Games are held in Sydney

The **SYDNEY HARBOUR BRIDGE** was built in 1932, and is the widest long-span bridge and tallest steel arch bridge in the world. It is also the 5th longest spanning-arch bridge according to *Guinness World Records*.

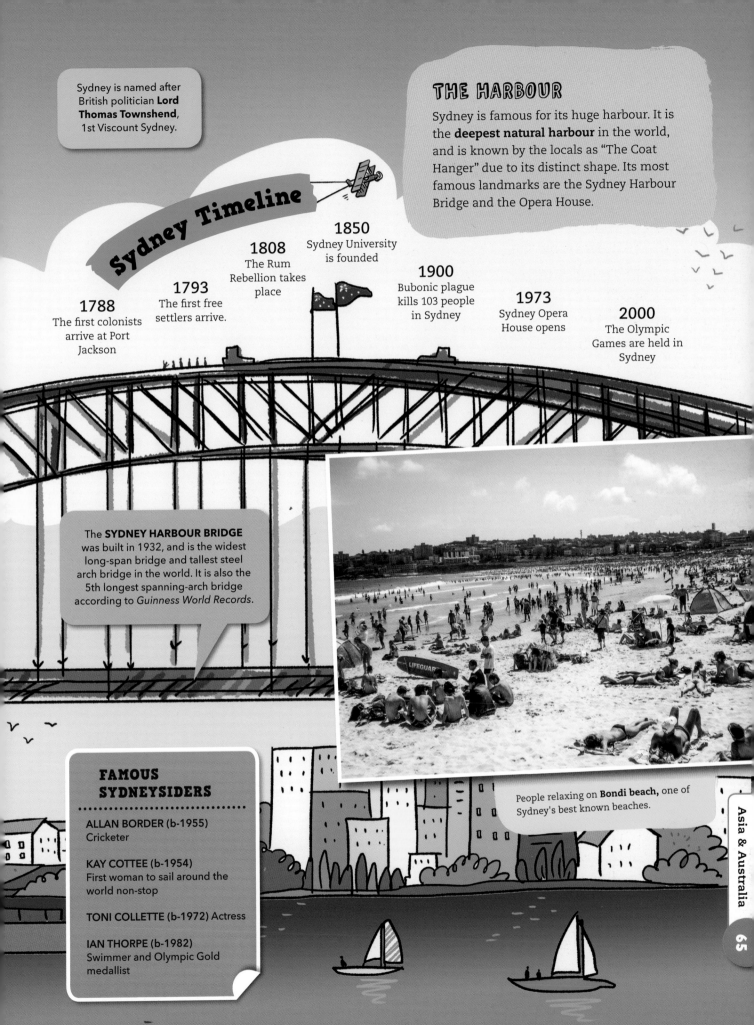

People relaxing on **Bondi beach,** one of Sydney's best known beaches.

FAMOUS SYDNEYSIDERS

ALLAN BORDER (b-1955)
Cricketer

KAY COTTEE (b-1954)
First woman to sail around the world non-stop

TONI COLLETTE (b-1972) Actress

IAN THORPE (b-1982)
Swimmer and Olympic Gold medallist

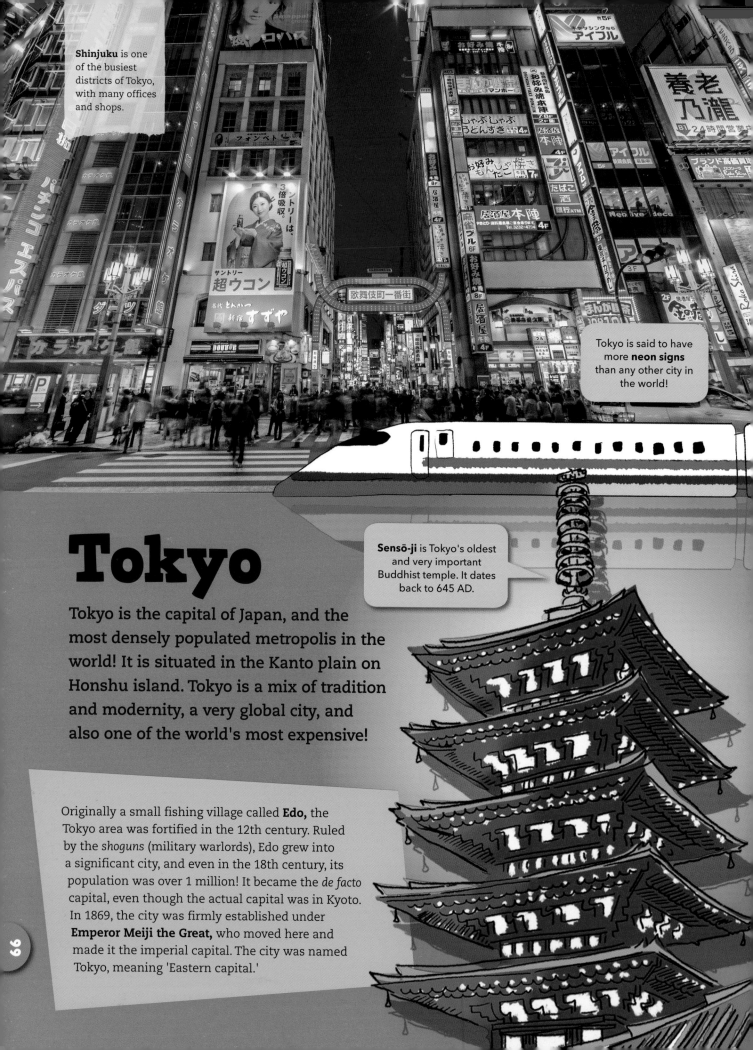

Shinjuku is one of the busiest districts of Tokyo, with many offices and shops.

Tokyo is said to have more **neon signs** than any other city in the world!

Tokyo

Tokyo is the capital of Japan, and the most densely populated metropolis in the world! It is situated in the Kanto plain on Honshu island. Tokyo is a mix of tradition and modernity, a very global city, and also one of the world's most expensive!

Sensō-ji is Tokyo's oldest and very important Buddhist temple. It dates back to 645 AD.

Originally a small fishing village called **Edo,** the Tokyo area was fortified in the 12th century. Ruled by the *shoguns* (military warlords), Edo grew into a significant city, and even in the 18th century, its population was over 1 million! It became the *de facto* capital, even though the actual capital was in Kyoto. In 1869, the city was firmly established under **Emperor Meiji the Great,** who moved here and made it the imperial capital. The city was named Tokyo, meaning 'Eastern capital.'

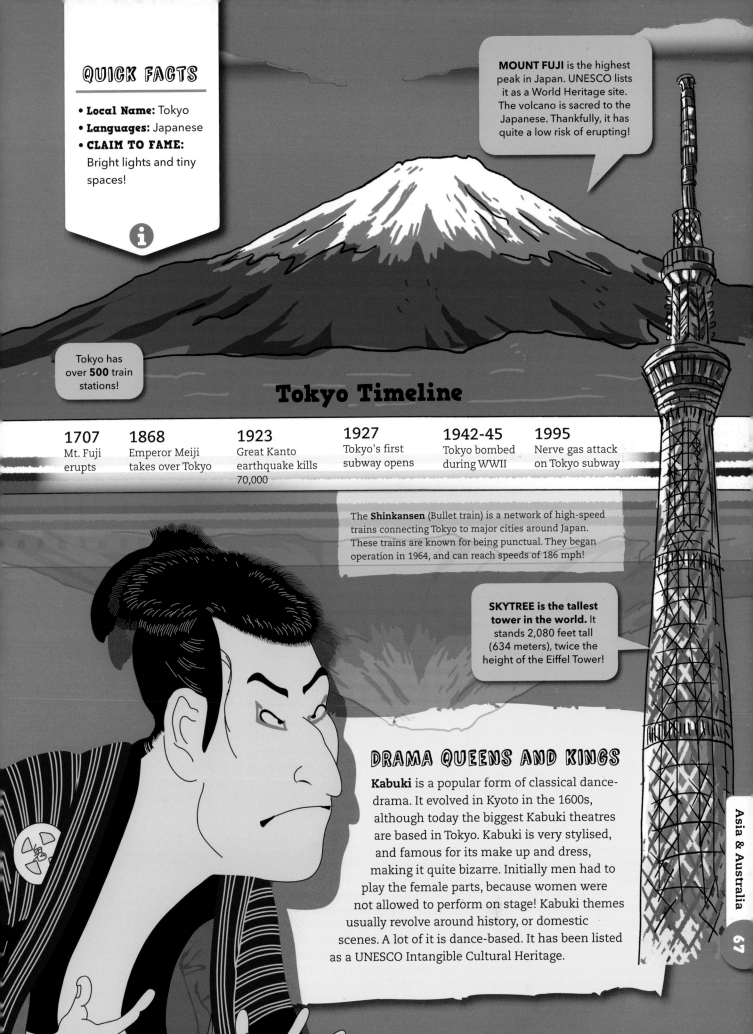

QUICK FACTS

- **Local Name:** Tokyo
- **Languages:** Japanese
- **CLAIM TO FAME:** Bright lights and tiny spaces!

MOUNT FUJI is the highest peak in Japan. UNESCO lists it as a World Heritage site. The volcano is sacred to the Japanese. Thankfully, it has quite a low risk of erupting!

Tokyo has over **500** train stations!

Tokyo Timeline

1707	1868	1923	1927	1942-45	1995
Mt. Fuji erupts	Emperor Meiji takes over Tokyo	Great Kanto earthquake kills 70,000	Tokyo's first subway opens	Tokyo bombed during WWII	Nerve gas attack on Tokyo subway

The **Shinkansen** (Bullet train) is a network of high-speed trains connecting Tokyo to major cities around Japan. These trains are known for being punctual. They began operation in 1964, and can reach speeds of 186 mph!

SKYTREE is the tallest tower in the world. It stands 2,080 feet tall (634 meters), twice the height of the Eiffel Tower!

DRAMA QUEENS AND KINGS

Kabuki is a popular form of classical dance-drama. It evolved in Kyoto in the 1600s, although today the biggest Kabuki theatres are based in Tokyo. Kabuki is very stylised, and famous for its make up and dress, making it quite bizarre. Initially men had to play the female parts, because women were not allowed to perform on stage! Kabuki themes usually revolve around history, or domestic scenes. A lot of it is dance-based. It has been listed as a UNESCO Intangible Cultural Heritage.

ANCHORAGE, ALASKA is the northernmost city in the United States.

VANCOUVER is a major industrial centre on the west coast of Canada.

ANTARCTIC OCEAN

MONTREAL is Canada's second biggest city, and has been named 'UNESCO City of Design.'

HUDSON BAY

SEATTLE, in Washington, is the fastest growing city in the US, and is known as a vibrant centre for music.

PHILADELPHIA, in Pennsylvania, is the historic city where America declared independence in 1776.

LAS VEGAS is famous for its leisure resorts. It is Nevada's major financial and cultural hub.

WASHINGTON, DC, is the capital of the US and home to its Federal Government and the Supreme Court.

ATLANTIC OCEAN

PACIFIC OCEAN

AUSTIN in Texas is the state capital, and known as 'The Live Music Capital of the World.'

HOUSTON, Texas, is the fourth most populated city in the US, and home to NASA's mission control centre.

MIAMI, in Florida, is one of the richest cities in the US and the world.

Great Cities of
NORTH AMERICA

Chicago

Chicago is the third largest city in the US. Originally the home of various American Indian tribes, it became a town in 1883. It rapidly developed into a centre of industry and transportation, helped by its location near the Chicago River and the Great Lakes.

QUICK FACTS

- **Local Name:** Chicago
- **Languages:** English
- **CLAIM TO FAME:** Modern architecture, and musical heritage

The nickname **WINDY CITY** comes from the fact that Chicago sits next to Lake Michigan and its cool breezes. However, some people say it comes from the idea that Chicagoans boast a lot about their city!

THE GREAT FIRE AND A NEW CITY

On October 8th, 1871, one Mrs. O' Leary lit a lantern in her barn at DeKoven Street. The story goes that her cow kicked the lantern, setting the barn - and most of Chicago - on fire! Because the buildings were mostly wooden, it caused a lot of damage, destroying one-third of the town and leaving almost 100,000 people homeless. Yet Chicago was able to reinvent itself with top speed. **The Great Rebuilding** led to modern architecture, a new urban centre and the rise of big business in the city.

CHICAGO BLUES

The city has an important musical history. A lot of African-American migrants arrived here in the 1900s to work in the industries. They brought their traditional music with them and Chicago developed its own style of **Blues** and **Jazz**. Soul and Gospel were also popular. Famous artists of that time include **Muddy Waters**, **Howlin' Wolf** and **Nat King Cole**.

FAMOUS CHICAGOANS

WALT DISNEY (1901-1966)
Animation film-maker.

BILL MURRAY (b-1950)
Actor and Comedian

HILLARY CLINTON (b-1947)
Politician

HARRISON FORD (b-1947)
Actor

BARACK OBAMA (b-1961)
44th US President, Senator from Illinois, resident of Chicago.

WILLIS TOWER (formerly known as the **Sears Tower**), is the second tallest building in the US. It was built in 1974 and stands 1451 ft. high.

TWO PRUDENTIAL PLAZA was finished in 1990 and has won many awards for its design.

THE CHICAGO SCHOOL

Chicago is famous for its architecture. Some of the world's first skyscrapers were built here. Buildings associated with the Chicago School of Architecture are modern in style, and often built on a steel frame.

The **JOHN HANCOCK CENTER** was built in 1969. It is built with a 'tubular' steel frame, which keeps it straight during an earthquake or heavy winds.

The **CRAIN COMMUNICATIONS BUILDING** was built in 1983 and has an unusual slanted facade.

Chicago Timeline

1674
Jacques Marquette builds the first dwelling at present-day Chicago.

1772-1773
Explorer Jean Baptiste-Pointe DuSable settles Chicago.

1809
Chicago becomes part of the Territory of Illinois.

1860 May 18
The Republican Party nominates Abraham Lincoln as candidate for presidency.

1871 October 8
The Great Fire rages for two days.

1900
The Chicago River is completely reversed.

1979
American Airlines Flight 191 crashes at O'Hare International Airport

Los Angeles

LA is located in the state of California, and is America's second most populous city after NYC. It is one of the most ethnically diverse places in the world, and with the best of media, culture, sports and technology, it is a truly global city.

When Los Angeles was founded in 1781, it was called **'El Pueblo de Nuestra Senora la Reina de Los Angeles de la Porciuncula'**, which translated to 'Town of Our Lady the Queen of the Angeles of the Small Portion'.

LA got the world's first parking meter in 1942!

HOLLYWOOD

Los Angeles is most famous for Hollywood, America's film and entertainment industry. There are many historic studios there. So is the **Hollywood Walk of Fame,** where stars leave their hand prints! A lot of these celebrities live in **Beverly Hills,** a separate city in LA County, which is also known just by its zip code, 90210. Many films and tv shows have been set in Beverly Hills. LA hosts the annual OSCARS™ (Academy Awards) every year.

LA Timeline

c.500 AD
Tongva Indians settle in Los Angeles basin.

1769
First Spanish settlement in the area.

1781
Group of 11 Mexican families settles by the river.

1848
Mexico formally cedes California to the US.

LA sits on the third-largest **oil field** in the US!

The Hollywood sign originally said 'HOLLYWOODLAND.'

YWOOD

1871
First rail link between Los Angeles and San Francisco.

1911
First Hollywood company, Nestor Film Company opens in LA.

1928
Walt Disney releases Steamboat Willie, starring Mickey Mouse.

1984
LA becomes the only US city to host the Olympics twice.

The famous **Griffith Observatory** was used to train pilots during World War II, so that they could navigate using the position of stars. Later, NASA astronauts on the Apollo missions were also trained here.

ON SHAKY GROUND!

Los Angeles sits on the San Andreas Fault. (Faults are caused by tectonic plates under the earth's surface, moving and hitting each other). The San Andreas Fault is caused by the Pacific Ring of Fire. This is a group of 450 volcanoes in the Pacific Ocean, which cause 90% of the world's earthquakes! California gets almost 10,000 minor earthquakes every year!

New York

New York City is one of the most famous cities in the world. Lying on the east coast of the USA, it is its most populous city. A cultural hotspot, it is home to many famous artists, writers, actors and musicians. NYC is also the financial centre of the USA. It has a vibrant, diverse population, and hundreds of different languages are spoken here!

QUICK FACTS

- **Local Name:** NYC
- **Languages:** Mainly English, amongst many others
- **CLAIM TO FAME:** Centre of the Universe!

THE FAMOUS SKYLINE

Manhattan is well-known for its skyline. It has some of the tallest buildings in the world, designed in many different styles by famous architects.

The **CHRYSLER BUILDING** is an Art Deco style skyscraper, built in 1931 and designed by William Van Alen. It has 77 floors and stands 319 metres tall!

8 SPRUCE STREET is a residential skyscraper, 265 metres tall and designed by Frank Gehry.

CITIGROUP CENTER is 279 metres tall, and was built in 1977 for Citibank.

The **EMPIRE STATE BUILDING** has 103 floors and is 443 metres tall. It was also designed in the Art Deco style by William Lamb.

The **METLIFE BUILDING** was built in 1963 in the International style.

ST. PATRICK'S CATHEDRAL is a landmark church built in 1878

1626 Dutch officer Peter Minuit buys the island of Manhattan from native Americans

1664 The English take over from the Dutch, naming the area New York

1785-1790 New York is the capital of the USA during these years when the Congress meets in the city

1860 The Great Irish Famine brings hunders of thousands of Irish immigrants to New York

2001 The World Trade Centre buildings are destroyed in a terrorist attack.

NICKNAMES FOR NYC

New York is also called:
- **THE BIG APPLE** (because of an old horse-racing tradition)
- The City of Lights
- The City of Dreams
- The Melting Pot

TIMES SQUARE is called the 'Crossroads of the World', because of its bright neon lights and bustling streets!

The **STATUE OF LIBERTY** was given as a gift by France in 1886. She arrived by ship in many pieces, and was assembled here. Lady Liberty greeted all new immigrants arriving on Ellis Island, (now called Liberty island), looking for a better life in America.

ONE WORLD TRADE CENTER is 103 floors and 541 metres high. It is part of the new World Trade Center complex.

The iconic **FLATIRON BUILDING** resembles an old clothes iron, and was built in 1902.

The **WOOLWORTH BUILDING,** was designed by Cass Gilbert in the Neo-Gothic style in 1913. It stands at 241 metres tall.

BROOKLYN BRIDGE was built in 1883 on the East River. It connects the boroughs of Manhattan and Brooklyn.

THE GUGGENHEIM is an art museum, designed by Frank Lloyd Wright and opened in 1959.

North America

75

SUPERHEROES

New York is the favourite city of comic book heroes. Over the years, it has been trampled by **Godzilla**, terrorised by **King Kong** and saved by **Batman. Superman,** a.k.a. Clark Kent, works as a reporter in Metropolis, based on New York. And **Spiderman,** a.k.a. Peter Parker, is a New York City teenager.

The American Museum of Natural History was founded in 1869. It is one of the world's biggest and most popular museums. Around 5 million people visit it every year! It has 45 permanent exhibition halls, including one for meteors, and another for fossils.

SPORTS IN NEW YORK CITY

New York is a sporting city. **The New York Yankees** and the **Mets** are famous major league baseball teams based here. The city is home ground for basketball teams the **New York Knicks** (men) and the **New York Liberty** (women). The ice hockey team for the city is called **NY Rangers.** It is also where the annual **U.S. Open Tennis** championships are played, at Flushing Meadows. **The New York Giants** and **Jets** play American football for the city, and the **Red Bulls** play European-style soccer. To top it all, almost 50,000 people run the annual **New York Marathon,** a gruelling 26 mile journey through all five boroughs! It is, of course, the world's largest marathon event.

THE YELLOW CAB

The taxicabs of New York are famous icons of the city. The yellow ones are called 'medallion cabs' and from 2013, there will be new green cabs called 'boro taxis.'

FAMOUS NEW YORKERS

WOODY ALLEN (b-1938)
Film director

MARIA CALLAS (1923-1977)
Opera singer

DUKE ELLINGTON (1899-1974)
Jazz pianist

GEORGE GERSHWIN (1898-1937)
Composer

ROBERT DE NIRO (b-1943)
Actor

RICHARD FEYNMAN (1918-1999)
Nobel Prize-winning physicist

WASHINGTON IRVING (1783-1859)
Author

HERMAN MELVILLE (1819-1891)
Author

MAURICE SENDAK (1928-2012)
Author and illustrator

BIG APPLE BITES...

New York is fast-paced city where everyone is in a hurry. Food-on-the-go is very popular, with the iconic hotdog stands selling a variety of quick bites. The city even has an award, called the Vendy, given each year to the best fast food cart!

Pizza

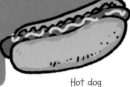
Hot dog

Pretzel

Donut

CENTRAL PARK

Manhattan's famous green spot, Central Park was first opened in 1857, and designed by Frederick Law Olmsted and Calvert Vaux.

The park is so big, it covers **6%** of Manhattan's total area!

There are almost **9000 benches** to sit on!

Central Park has more than **26,000 trees**, and more than **200 species** of birds!

The park is home to **29 sculptures**, including one of *Alice in Wonderland*.

Around **250 films** have been shot here, making Central Park the most filmed public park in the world!

Around **30 million** people visit the park every year!

San Francisco

'The City by the Bay,' is known for its scenic beauty as well as its cosmopolitan atmosphere. It is located on the California coast, surrounded by estuaries and bays. San Francisco holds a special place in popular culture, attracting writers and artistes to its laid-back vibe.

QUICK FACTS

- **Local Name:** SF, San Fran
- **Languages:** English
- **CLAIM TO FAME:** Natural beauty, and the Tech industry

GOLDEN CITY

The area was originally inhabited by the Ohlone/Costanoan Indians. The Spanish arrived and settled here in 1769. They established the *Mission San Francisco de Asís*, or **Mission Dolores.** Many years later, army officer and explorer John C. Frémont named the strait that connects San Francisco to the Pacific Ocean the **Golden Gate.** This name was adopted for the iconic bridge that was later built across the strait.

THE ROCK

In the San Francisco Bay stands **Alcatraz Island.** It was first used to house a lighthouse for the bay. Then it was used as a military fort. Between 1934 and 1963, the island was a maximum-security prison, and housed some of America's most notorious criminals. Some famous inmates included gangster Al Capone, and murderer Robert "Birdman of Alcatraz" Stroud. No prisoner ever escaped **'the Rock,'** as Alcatraz was called, although some did try their luck!

The city's cable cars are the only US **National Historical Monument** that can move!

Poet Lawrence Ferlinghetti opened the landmark **'City Lights Bookstore'** in 1953, because he wanted to give the **'BEAT'** writers a voice in San Francisco.

San Francisco Timeline

1776
Spanish colonists found *Mission Dolores*

1847
Yerba Buena renamed "San Francisco"

1848
California ceded from Mexico to the United States

1849
Gold Rush begins

1850
San Francisco becomes a city

1906
San Francisco is devastated by earthquake and fire

1937
Golden Gate Bridge opens

1945
United Nations Charter is signed at historic conference in the city

BOOMTOWN

Between 1848 and 1855 gold was discovered in California. Over 300,000 people rushed here to "strike it rich". San Francisco was a small town of around 1,000 people then, but soon grew to over 30,000 residents. More than 90,000 gold-diggers came from around the world, not just America. These people were called the Forty-Niners, after the year 1849. Because of the gold rush, San Francisco became known as a 'boomtown'.

The Spanish first called San Francisco **Yerba Buena,** meaning 'good herb,' after a medicinal plant found here.

The **Golden Gate Bridge** connects San Francisco to Marin County. It is one of the most beautiful bridges in the world, and when it opened in 1937, it was also the longest suspension bridge.

FAMOUS SAN FRANCISCANS

ROBERT LEE FROST (1874-1963)
Poet

JACK LONDON (1876-1916)
Novelist and writer

ANSEL ADAMS (1902-1984)
Photographer

CLINT EASTWOOD (b. 1930)
Actor and Director

STEVE JOBS (1955-2011)
Entrepreneur and founder of Apple Inc.

The US Navy originally wanted to paint the Golden Gate bridge in **yellow and black stripes,** for better visibility!

San Francisco is famous for the blanket fog that covers it on some mornings!

Toronto

Toronto is the largest city in Canada, and the capital of Ontario province. It was was first settled by the Seneca tribe of American Indians, and later colonised by the French and the British. Today it is the fourth largest city in North America, and Canada's greatest city for commerce and culture.

QUICK FACTS

- **Local Name:** Toronto
- **Languages:** English, Chinese, Italian among others
- **CLAIM TO FAME:** A very multicultural city!

Traders and missionaries first arrived here in the 1600s. It was the French who first used the name Toronto, when they built fortifications in the 1700s. However they were soon defeated by the British, who annexed Canada. They named the town York. In 1834, the town became a city, and was renamed Toronto. When railways were built in the 1850s, there was a large influx of migrants and war refugees from all corners of the world.

The Canadian National Tower is an icon of Toronto, and was the tallest tower in the world for 34 years.

In 1880, the famous poet **Walt Whitman** described Toronto as "a lively, dashing place".

The campus of **OCAD University** (formerly the Ontario College of Art and Design), is located in Toronto. This modernist extension, called the A. J. Casson Wing, was opened in 1957.

Toronto has the **largest underground pedestrian system** in the world, connecting 1200 stores and restaurants and 50 offices.

Toronto hosts the **Caribana,** the biggest Caribbean street celebration in North America.

FAMOUS TORONTONIANS

MARGARET ATWOOD (b-1939)
Booker Prize-winning novelist, poet

FRANK GEHRY (b-1929)
Pritzker Prize-winning architect

ROHINTON MISTRY (b-1952)
Novelist and writer

JONI MITCHELL (b-1943)
Singer songwriter

FREDERICK BANTING (1891-1941)
Scientist and co-discoverer of Insulin, 1923 Nobel Laureate

CULTURE AND MULTICULTURE...

Toronto is one of the most ethnically diverse cities in the world. Almost half the people living in Toronto are foreign-born! Many people of British origin, as well as Chinese and Indian, live there. It is also a city famous for its vibrant culture, with numerous museums, festivals, sports events and theatres. Musicians, writers and artists thrive in Toronto. A lot of literature has been set here, including books by Margaret Atwood and Michael Ondaatje. Toronto also hosts the most film festivals in the world!

Toronto's **Royal Ontario Museum** is known around the world. The museum opened in 1914. Its new main entrance, the **Crystal,** is a glass and aluminium structure was designed by Daniel Libeskind, and opened in 2007.

Toronto Timeline

1500 - 1793
Iroquois people inhabit the area

1793
JG Simcoe establishes town of York

1813
Battle of York, town captured by US Forces

1834
Toronto reverts to its native name

1837
Unsuccessful rebellion against the British government

1845 - 1852
Irish migrants arrive, to escape famine at home

1904
Great fire of Toronto

2010
Toronto hosts G-20 Summit

Toronto is the **most populous** city in Canada.

Mexico City

Mexico City is the capital of Mexico and of its industry, culture, and education. It is the oldest city in North America, founded first as the Aztec capital in 1325 and rebuilt as a modern city by the Spanish. Mexico City attracts people from all over the country, many of whom have both a Native American and European heritage.

QUICK FACTS

- **Local Name:** Ciudad de México
- **Languages:** Spanish
- **CLAIM TO FAME:** Capital of the great Aztec culture.

One-fifth of the urban Mexican population lives in Mexico City.

THE AZTECS

The legend goes that Tenoch, a priest, had a vision for a sacred place, marked by 'an eagle eating a snake, perched on a cactus'. As the Aztecs wandered the Mexico Valley, they saw this sight on an island of Lake Texcoco. So here, around 1325, they founded **Tenochtitlán: 'Place of the High Priest Tenoch'.** The city rapidly expanded, farming flourished, and the military grew powerful. By the 16th century, the city had nearly 200,000 inhabitants.

Emperor Moctezuma II, depicted in the *Tovar Manuscript*, which narrates the history of the Aztecs.

FAMOUS CHILANGOS

OCTAVIO PAZ (1914-1998), Poet, Author

FRIDA KAHLO (1907-1954), Painter

MARIO MOLINA (b. 1943), Winner of a Nobel Prize in 1995, for research on the ozone layer.

HOT CHOCOLATE!

Chocolate originated in the Andes mountains of Central America, where cocoa trees can thrive. Even around 2000 BC, people in Mexico were grinding the cocoa beans to make a drink. Sometimes they added honey, and sometimes chillies. They called it 'xocolatl' meaning bitter drink. All indigenous Central Americans, including the Mayans and the Aztecs, loved chocolate. By the 1400s, the Aztecs had even put a tax on chocolate. When the Spanish brought it to Europe, sugar was added to it, and the world has loved it ever since!

Mexico City is the richest city in Latin America!

This is the largest **Spanish-speaking** city in the world.

Mexico City Timeline

1325
Tenochtitlán founded by Aztecs

1521
City destroyed by Spanish forces

1824
Mexico City made capital of independent Mexico

1847
US troops capture city during Mexican-American War

1968
Mexico City hosts the Olympics

1985
Massive earthquake kills 10,000

1997
Cuauhtémoc Cárdenas becomes first city mayor to be elected by the people.

When the Spanish arrived in 1519, they were impressed by the Aztec capital. **Hernan Cortes,** conquistador and leader of the Spanish expedition, did everything he could to conquer Tenochtitlán. The Spanish were welcomed by the Aztec emperor, **Moctezuma II,** but they took him prisoner. In 1520, Moctezuma was killed. The Spanish destroyed Tenochtitlán, and built a new city to symbolise their dominion over the New World. The Spanish conquest of Mexico is one of the most important events in world history.

Mexico later won its independence from Spain in 1821. Mexico City was also the scene of intense fighting during the Mexican Revolution (1910–20).

HAVANA, capital city of Cuba, an eclectic and culturally unique society, and a diverse economy.

CARACAS, capital and largest city of Venezuela. Cosmopolitan city known for its cuisine.

BOGOTA is the capital of Columbia, an historic, yet modern metropolis.

PACIFIC OCEAN

ATLANTIC OCEAN

LIMA is the capital of Peru. An important industrial and financial hub in Latin America.

SÃO PAULO, the largest city in Brazil, and a multi cultural melting-pot of 20 million people.

SANTIAGO is the capital and largest city of Chile, surrounded by snowy Andean mountains.

MONTEVIDEO is the capital and largest city of Uruguay, with a rich cultural heritage.

Great Cities of

SOUTH AMERICA

Buenos Aires

Buenos Aires is Argentina's capital, and its most populous city. It started out as a major port, and grew into one of the most important cities in South America. It is said that the history of Buenos Aires is the history of Argentina itself.

QUICK FACTS

- **Local Name:** Buenos Aires
- **Languages:** Buenos Aires' Spanish
- **CLAIM TO FAME:** The Tango and the European-style architecture

1 in 4 Argentines live in Buenos Aires!

Avenida de Mayo is named for the May Revolution of 1810, which led to Argentina's independence.

Argentines speak Spanish with a different accent. Their language is peppered with **Lunfardo,** which is a special type of slang, developed in Buenos Aires.

GRAND ARCHITECTURE

Buenos Aires is often called the **"Paris of South America."** And no wonder, because its architecture and atmosphere are symbols of a prosperous and elegant history. The city is full of grand *Neoclassical* and *Art Nouveau* buildings.

The majestic **Avenida de Mayo** was Buenos Aires' first boulevard. It contains many plazas, sculptures and monuments. At one end of the boulevard stands the presidential palace, Casa Rosada, and at the other end the National Congress. So every time Argentina's president goes to work, he uses this very road.

FAMOUS PORTEÑOS

BERNARDO ALBERTO HOUSSAY (1887-1971)
Physiologist, Nobel laureate for medicine

DIEGO MARADONA (1960)
Footballer, 1986 World Cup winner for Argentina

GABRIELA SABATINI (b-1970)
Tennis player and Women's US Open champion

Buenos Aires Timeline

1539
Indigenous tribes drive out Spanish settlers from Buenos Aires area.

1580
Spaniard Juan de Garay establishes a city, named Trinidad

1806-7
Britain attempts to invade the city.

1853
City becomes capital of State of Buenos Aires.

1955
Bombing of Plaza de Mayo in a failed coup

Buenos Aires means **'Good Airs'** or **'Fair Winds'** in Spanish.

La Boca is a *barrio* (district) in Buenos Aires. This colourful area is home to artists and musicians.

TANGO

This world-famous form of music and dance began in *Rio de la Plata* in the 19th century. Argentines enjoy this rhythm in the cafes and bars of Buenos Aires. The dance itself is inspired by African and European cultures. It is so important to the region, that UNESCO includes it in its list of **Intangible Cultural Heritage!**

The inhabitants of the city are called *porteños,* because the port was so vital to the development of both Buenos Aires, and Argentina.

Rio de Janeiro

Rio de Janeiro is the second largest city in Brazil. It is also the capital city of the State of Rio de Janeiro. Founded in the 16th century by the Portuguese, it was the country's capital for almost two hundred years. Today Rio is still considered the cultural heart of Brazil because of its history, architecture, music and art.

QUICK FACTS

- **Local Name:** Rio
- **Languages:** Portuguese
- **CLAIM TO FAME:** Fantastic beaches, and Christ the Redeemer

RIVER? WHAT RIVER?

In January 1501, Portuguese explorer Gaspar de Lemos arrived at the huge Guanabara Bay. Mistaking the bay for a river, he named it Rio de Janeiro, which means 'January River' in Portuguese! At the time the area was inhabited by the *Botocudo*, *Tupi*, *Puri*, and *Maxakalí* indigenous peoples. The Portuguese returned in 1565 to found the city , which was then named **São Sebastião do Rio de Janeiro** in honour of the King of Portugal, Dom Sebastião.

FOOTBALL!

Football, or soccer, is the most popular sport in Brazil. The state of Rio de Janeiro alone has four teams: Botafogo, Flamengo, Fluminense and Vasco da Gama. Rio's huge Maracanã stadium hosts the most important games, and it is where the 2014 World Cup games were played.

The iconic **SUGAR LOAF MOUNTAIN** is very popular with rock-climbers from around the world!

Rio will become the first city in Latin America to host the **OLYMPICS,** in 2016.

The Cariocas enjoy cycling. Rio has bike paths all along its beaches.

Rio de Janeiro is also called **CIDADE MARAVILHOSA,** which means 'The Marvellous City'.

Rio's beaches are famous around the world. Some popular ones are **IPANEMA, COPACABANA** and **LEBLON**.

Rio is also famous for its **Carnival**, known as 'the world's largest party'. Thousands of people go dancing and singing down the *Sambódromo*, a street built just to host the Carnival parade.

FAVELAS are 'slums' where traditionally the city's poor used to live. Nowadays they house a mix of people, and are like cities within a city. Rio itself has around 600 favelas, **Rocinha** being the largest.

Rio Timeline

1565
Rio de Janeiro founded by the Portuguese.

763
Portuguese empire's capital moved to Rio from Salvador.

1822
City becomes capital of independent Brazil.

1877
Santa Teresa Tram, one of the oldest in the world, starts operation.

1923
The famous Copacabana Palace Hotel opens.

1958
Brazil win the football World Cup for the first time.

1960
Brazilian capital moves from Rio to Brasília.

The famous **CHRIST THE REDEEMER** on Corcovado mountain, is the second largest statue of Christ in the world. Designed by sculptor Paul Landowski, it opened in 1931.

FAMOUS CARIOCAS

RONALDO (b-1976)
Football player for Brazil and Real Madrid.

TOM JOBIM (1927-1994)
Composer and musician, known for Jazz and *Bossa Nova* music.

OSCAR NIEMEYER (1907-2012)
Architect known for his modern designs. He helped in the planning of **Brasilia**, Brazil's capital city.

The **TIJUCA RAINFOREST** is a massive urban forest on the mountains surrounding Rio. It was declared a National Park in 1961.

CASABLANCA, largest city Morocco, and one of the most economically vibrant cities of Africa.

LUXOR, ancient capital of Egypt, famous for its temple complexes.

MARRAKECH is the cultural heart of Morocco and an important former imperial city.

MEDITERRANEAN SEA

ACCRA is the capital and largest city of Ghana, and a major financial centre.

NAIROBI, the capital and largest city of Kenya, also known as the *Green City in the Sun.*

LAGOS is the fastest growing city in Nigeria. and a major port.

SOUTH ATLANTIC OCEAN

INDIAN OCEAN

CAPE TOWN, second-largest city of South Africa, and legislative capital of the country.

Great Cities of

AFRICA

Cairo

Cairo is Egypt's capital, and the largest city in Africa. Egyptians call it Al-Qahira. It is a really old city, dating back to the 7th century AD. It was built on the banks of the mighty river Nile, and is famous for its ancient Pyramids. Today, Cairo is a modern city with a huge population.

QUICK FACTS

- **Local Name:** Al Qahira
- **Languages:** Arabic, English and French.
- **CLAIM TO FAME:** Land of Pharaohs and pyramids!

Cairo is also called the **CITY OF 1000 MINARETS!** The people of Cairo are called Cairenes.

THE MIGHTY PYRAMIDS

Almost every pyramid in Egypt is located near Cairo! This is because modern Cairo sits very near the ancient Egyptian capital, Memphis. **The Great Pyramid of Giza** was built around 2540 BC as a tomb for a Pharaoh called Khufu. Standing 137 metres high, for almost 4000 years it was the tallest building in the world. It is also the oldest of the Ancient Wonders of the world yet, surprisingly, it is almost intact today!

The **GREAT SPHINX** of Giza is a mythical figure of a lion with a man's head. It is the oldest known large sculpture in the world, built around 2540 BC. It is also the world's biggest monolithic (carved from a single piece of rock) statue!

Cairo is home to Egypt's oldest university, called **AL-AZHAR UNIVERSITY**, founded in the 10th Century.

FELUCCA are traditional river boats, used in ancient Egypt and still cruising on the Nile today.

The famous funeral mask of King Tut

CAIRO TIMELINE

3000 BC - 200 AD
The pyramids are built at Giza and other sites around present-day Cairo. Memphis, south of Giza, was an important city at the time.

200 - 640
Greeks and Romans took over as the Pharoahs declined, founding Babylon on the current site of Cairo.

640-969 CE
The Muslims invaded Egypt and set up the city of Al-Fustat near Babylon. Al Fustat was the capital for 200 years.

969 - 1517
The Egyptians had a stable and prosperous phase under the **Mamluks,** who encouraged trade, art and education.

1517 -1805
The Ottomans invaded and plundered Cairo, ruling it from far-away Turkey.

Modern Cairo
A revolution in 1952 ends the British occupation of Egypt. Cairo becomes a **modern metropolis,** first under Muhammad Ali and then under Khedive Ismail Pasha.

TREASURE TROVE
The Egyptian Museum of Antiquities contains many important pieces of ancient Egyptian history. It has the world's largest collection of artefacts from the time of the pharaohs, and many treasures of King Tutankhamen.

DOWNTOWN CAIRO is the the urban centre of Cairo city. Khedive Ismail asked for it to be designed in a modern, European style, because he liked the architecture in Paris.

In 2011, Tahrir Square in downtown Cairo became the focus of a major public uprising, or revolution, which led to the government's fall.

FAMOUS CAIRENES

BOUTROS BOUTROS GHALI, Secretary General of the United Nations (UN) from 1992 to 1996, was born in Cairo in 1922.

GAMAL ABDEL NASSER was the second **President of Egypt,** from 1956 to 1970. He was a progressive politician, who helped overthrow the monarchy. Nasser was born in Alexandria, Egypt, but his political career was based in Cairo.

THE LIFELINE OF EGYPT
The Nile is the world's longest river, and is very important to the Egyptians. The papyrus reeds growing on its banks were used to make paper in ancient Egypt. Being next to the Nile helped Cairo develop into a major port city, and the city was very important to the spice trade between the East and the West in the 13th century.

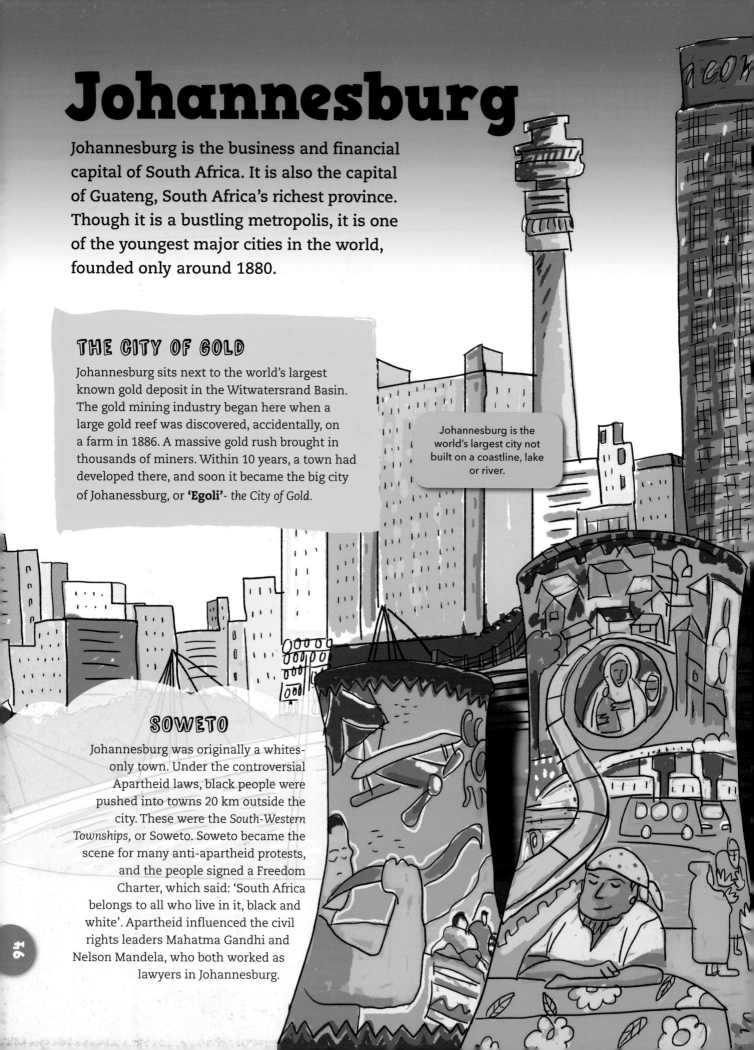

Johannesburg

Johannesburg is the business and financial capital of South Africa. It is also the capital of Guateng, South Africa's richest province. Though it is a bustling metropolis, it is one of the youngest major cities in the world, founded only around 1880.

THE CITY OF GOLD

Johannesburg sits next to the world's largest known gold deposit in the Witwatersrand Basin. The gold mining industry began here when a large gold reef was discovered, accidentally, on a farm in 1886. A massive gold rush brought in thousands of miners. Within 10 years, a town had developed there, and soon it became the big city of Johanessburg, or **'Egoli'**- *the City of Gold*.

Johannesburg is the world's largest city not built on a coastline, lake or river.

SOWETO

Johannesburg was originally a whites-only town. Under the controversial Apartheid laws, black people were pushed into towns 20 km outside the city. These were the *South-Western Townships*, or Soweto. Soweto became the scene for many anti-apartheid protests, and the people signed a Freedom Charter, which said: 'South Africa belongs to all who live in it, black and white'. Apartheid influenced the civil rights leaders Mahatma Gandhi and Nelson Mandela, who both worked as lawyers in Johannesburg.

QUICK FACTS

- **Local Name:** Jo'burg
- **Languages:** English, Zulu, Afrikaans, Xhosa
- **CLAIM TO FAME:** Symbol of South Africa's journey to Democracy!

FAMOUS JOHANNESBURGERS

PHILLIP TOBIAS (1925-2012)
Palaentologist known for his work on the *Hominid* sites.

WINNIE MANDELA (b. 1937)
ANC activist and politician.

DAVE MATTHEWS (b.1967)
Actor and musician, now based in the US.

Joburg Timeline

100 AD
Inhabited by indigenous San and Bantu peoples

1800s
Dutch pioneers arrive in area

1886
Johannesburg township established by Boer government, after discovery of gold

1887
Johannesburg Stock Exchange founded

1900
Town captured by British forces during the Second Boer War

1961
City becomes part of the Republic of South Africa

2002
Soweto becomes part of city

2013
Nelson Mandela dies

Outside Johanessburg is a World Heritage site known as the **Cradle of Humankind**. Archaelogically, it is the world's richest **HOMININ** site, with around 40% of the world's human ancestor fossils found here.

Jo'burg is Africa's second largest global city, after Cairo.

KWAITO, catchy African house music, evolved in Jo'burg in the 90s and is very popular here.

Johannesburg has over **10 million trees,** and is also known as the largest man made forest in the world.

NELSON MANDELA

Mandela was born into the royal Tembu family, as Rolihlahla Mandela. He was given the name Nelson by his English teacher. Mandela lived in Soweto for many years, and was often jailed for his anti-Apartheid protests. In 1964 he was given a life sentence, but he was finally freed in 1990 after a long campaign for his release. In 1991 Mandela and the **African National Congress** (ANC) negotiated for majority-rule democracy in South Africa. Mandela, and the country's president FW de Klerk, shared the **Nobel Peace Prize** for ending Apartheid.

About the Author:

Charles Conway is a writer with a passion for travel and adventure. His writing has been featured in a range of print and digital publications and he has launched his own online platform for ethical travel. In between writing, Charles is developing his interest in prehistoric archaeology and can sometimes be found wandering the Bronze Age barrows and landscapes of West Sussex.

About the Illustrator:

Supriya Sahai has designed and illustrated for various publishers since 2001, including Dorling Kindersley, Lonely Planet, National Geographic, HarperCollins, Scholastic, Macmillan and Bloomsbury.

www.squareandcircus.co.uk